SATI
SAVITRI

SATI SAVITRI
AND OTHER FEMINIST TALES
THEY DON'T TELL YOU

Devdutt Pattanaik is the author of over fifty books and 1000 articles on the relevance of mythology in modern times. Trained in medicine, he worked in the health-care and pharmaceutical industries for fifteen years before devoting all his time to his passion for decoding beliefs of all cultures, modern and ancient, located beneath the veneer of rationality. He lives in Mumbai. To know more, visit www.devdutt.com.

Also by the Author

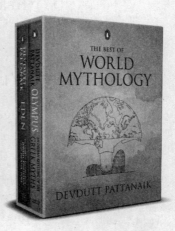

DEVDUTT PATTANAIK

INDIA'S BESTSELLING MYTHOLOGIST

SHIKHANDI

AND OTHER QUEER TALES THEY DON'T TELL YOU

SATI SAVITRI

AND OTHER FEMINIST STORIES THEY DON'T TELL YOU

DEVDUTT PATTANAIK

ILLUSTRATIONS BY THE AUTHOR

PENGUIN BOOKS

An imprint of Penguin Random House

PENGUIN BOOKS

Penguin Books is an imprint of the Penguin Random House group of companies whose addresses can be found at global.penguinrandomhouse.com

Published by Penguin Random House India Pvt. Ltd
4th Floor, Capital Tower 1, MG Road,
Gurugram 122 002, Haryana, India

Penguin
Random House
India

First published in Penguin Books by Penguin Random House India 2024

Text and illustrations copyright © Devdutt Pattanaik 2024

Illustrations by Devdutt Pattanaik

ISBN 9780143467588

Layout and design by Dhaivat Chhaya
Typeset in Book Antiqua by Special Effects Graphics Design Company, Mumbai
Printed at Replika Press Pvt. Ltd, India

www.penguin.co.in

FSC
www.fsc.org
MIX
Paper from
responsible sources
FSC® C016779

To my mother Sabitri
And to my father Prafulla, who adored her as his Lakshmi

Contents

Introduction

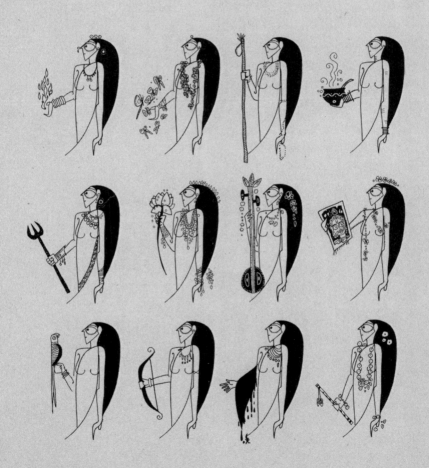

Mythology is a cultural truth expressed through stories, symbols and rituals.

- Western myth states that humans live only once.
- Indian myth states that all organisms live many lives.

When you live many lives, then gender becomes the result of karma, the outcome of deeds in our previous lives. All men have been women in past lives or will be women in future lives. All women have been men in past lives and will be men in future lives. Such ideas do not exist in the Western world. There is no explanation offered for why someone is male or female in Western myth. So it feels like an imposition.

Indian myth, in this book, means Hindu, Buddhist and Jain myths, whose stories, symbols and rituals originated in the Indian subcontinent (South Asia). Western myth means myths whose stories, symbols and rituals originated in lands to the west of India: not simply Europe and America, but also the Middle East, though not Africa. West also refers to the mindset that views progress as linear, from polytheism through monotheism to atheism.

The West's obsession with debate, the West's need to evangelize its particular truth as universal truth, i.e., the Truth, reveals that structurally it is a world view that is still storm-tossed between Greek polytheism and Middle Eastern (Biblical) monotheism. Both believed we live only once.

- Greek polytheism saw humans as potential threats to gods who kept them in check by distracting them with labour and wars.

- Biblical monotheism saw humans as petulant beings unable to willingly submit to God's law and love.

From Greek mythology comes the story of Pandora.

The Olympian gods were afraid that men would overthrow them, just as they had overthrown the Titans long ago. So they sent a woman called Pandora to distract the men. They gave Pandora a box with express instructions not to open it. They knew well that her curious nature would make her open the box in the land of men. And that is exactly what happened. Pandora opened the box and out came all the things that plague the world of men: jealousy, frustration, pride, greed, sloth. Thus distracted, men did not seek to fight or overthrow the Olympians. Greek mythology thus blames all the problems of the world upon women, the daughters of Pandora.

From Biblical mythology comes the story of Eve.

God created the world full of stars, planets, plants and animals. In this perfect world known as Eden, he created the first man and woman, Adam and Eve, with express instructions not to eat the fruit of one particular tree. But a serpent tempted Eve to disobey. She ate the fruit and got Adam to eat it as well. For this act of disobedience, Adam and Eve were cast out of Eden. They were the first humans. Their children would struggle and suffer on earth on account of the Original Sin, the first act of disobedience.

Both mythologies blame women for life's problems. Both mythologies present dominant male figures (Biblical God, Greek gods) as oppressors. We do not find equivalent tales in Hindu, Buddhist and Jain mythologies, which originated in India. Divinity in Hinduism manifests in male as well as female form. God is often presented as a couple, as husband and wife, in domestic harmony. There are even tales where women challenge the authority of men.

But Indian society is also patriarchal. Here, it is assumed that only beings with a male body can break free from the wheel of rebirths, not those with a female body. What stories contributed to the patriarchy in India? Are there Indian myths that challenged patriarchy in India? Can traditional stories that challenge male hegemony be qualified as feminist? Or is feminism only a post-industrial phenomenon, imported from the West?

The role of women in Indian mythology increases over time, with marginal roles in the older Vedic texts (1000 BC) and dominant roles in later Tantrik texts (1000 AD). This suggests a shift in thinking—with women asserting themselves into the mainstream discourse. From eighth century onwards, Buddhist art includes the female deity Tara as the embodiment of wisdom and compassion. In Jain art, we find powerful female goddesses, known as the yakshi, guarding the Tirthankara. In Hindu temples, there is no Shiva without Uma, no Vishnu without Lakshmi, no Ram without Sita, no Krishna without Radha. This book presents stories from this transition.

In these stories, women are not subservient to men. Their roles are not defined by men. They are not just wives, daughters, sisters and mothers. They are humans, wrapped in female flesh, who ask foundational questions about hierarchy, consent, choice and freedom. The male yearning to dominate and be territorial is seen not as a gender trait, but rather as a trait of the ego (*aham*), which eclipses the soul (*atma*). It feels like spiritual discourse in feminist clothing.

Devdutt Pattanaik

In modern mythology, all things traditional are oppressive. Tradition is patriarchy. Feminism is modernity. In postmodern mythology, every powerful person (privileged heterosexual males) is the oppressor, a patron of patriarchy.

- Is there a way to look at traditional lore without the modern or postmodern lens of judgement, without presupposing the world to be full of oppressors and the oppressed?

- Is it possible to find ideas, unique to India, that are often airbrushed when scholars homogenize and universalize the world of patriarchy? Can such an exercise not be seen as being defensive or apologetic about Indian culture?

- Can both men and women be simply seen as humans, hungry and frightened, coping with the world, and with life, unable to shed the burden of biology or privilege or culture?

This book retells popular Hindu, Buddhist and Jain myths with these questions in mind. So approach the stories in this book with curiosity, rather than combatively, keeping in mind:

Within infinite myths is an eternal truth
Who sees it all?
Varuna has but a thousand eyes.
Indra, a hundred
You and I, only two

Devdutt Pattanaik

1

Wives Who Rescue

Clay images of bejewelled women have been found in Harappa. They wore bangles made of conch-shells and probably even red sindoor in the parting of hair, as married women still do today.

Sati is both a proper noun and a common noun.

- As a proper noun, it refers to Sati, the first wife of Shiva, who killed herself by jumping into a Vedic fire altar and was reborn as his second wife, Parvati. Her story is explored in the chapter on Uma.

- As a common noun, sati refers to the practice of widows, mostly from warrior clans, who burnt themselves on the funeral pyres of their husbands.

- As a common noun, sati has another meaning. It is the title given to a chaste and faithful wife whose chastity and fidelity grant her magical powers to protect her husband, manipulate nature and even curse the gods.

People often confuse the three: the goddess, the historical practice and the mythological concept. Sati is simultaneously a violent practice and a glamorous idea that seeks to modify women's behaviour. It reveals how the well-being of the husband and prosperity of her household was transformed into a function of woman's fidelity. A man was luckiest if he secured a sati for a wife.

The Vedas, Hinduism's oldest scriptures, do not refer to Sati or sati. They speak of a widow lying next to the dead body of her husband who was then asked to rise up and return to the world of the living by grasping the hand of a new husband. Ancient Greeks spoke of this Indian practice in north-west India over 2000 years ago. Epics like the Mahabharata speak of queens like Madri, and even the wives of Krishna, who follow this practice. Many have argued that these are later interpolations.

It is only from the fifth to fifteenth centuries, across Kashmir, Maharashtra, Odisha, Andhra Pradesh, Telangana, Karnataka, Tamil Nadu, that we find 'sati' stones, venerating women who burnt themselves on the funeral pyre of their husbands. Such stones exist alongside 'vira' stones, commemorating the violent death of heroes who fought raiders or wild animals, and 'nishidhi' stones, commemorating the death-by-fasting of Jain monks. These were times when voluntary death evoked awe and veneration. Those who died in this manner were equated with gods.

The practice of burning widows, glamorized in traditional lore, is illegal today. Colonial missionaries of the eighteenth century over-exaggerated the incidence of widow burning to project India as a barbaric place. Traditionalists tend to downplay it and sometimes argue that it was a necessary practice to prevent the abuse of widows by foreign invaders.

The idea of women choosing to burn themselves on their husband's funeral pyre may have gained currency because in traditional Hindu society a widow (*vidhava*) had lower status than a woman whose husband was alive (*sadhava*). Even today, the housewife with husband and children is considered auspicious (*suhagan*) and is invited to participate in Hindu weddings, festivals and fertility rituals. She is seen as lucky (*sow-bhagya*), the harbinger of success (*su-mangali*). If she dies before her husband, she is considered the eternal bride (*sada-suhagan*). Her corpse is bedecked as a goddess, with red and gold, before being cremated. By contrast, a widow is deemed unlucky (*abhaga*). She loses status, privileges and agency.

Widows, especially in elite families, were not allowed to remarry and were forced to live spiritual lives, bereft of any material pleasures, almost making them regret not killing themselves on their husband's funeral pyre. This was done to ensure the widow did not claim her husband's property or shame his memory. She was equated with a fallow field that no other shall sow. To keep their status as sadhava, many Hindu women retell the story of Savitri, a determined and intelligent woman who was able to save her husband from the clutches of death.

Savitri was a princess, so educated that no prince wanted to marry her. So her father told her to choose her own husband. She chose to marry a woodcutter named Satyavan. Her father opposed the marriage but in the end relented, because it was her choice. An astrologer said that Satyavan's chosen husband would die at the end of the year. Savitri still did not change her mind about Satyavan. It was a happy marriage. But at the end of the year, Satyavan died. Savitri could see Yama, god of death, approach and pull out the breath from her husband's body. She left the lifeless body and began following Yama as he made his way to the land of the dead. Yama noticed her following him. 'Go back,' he said, 'and perform the funeral rituals.' But Savitri continued following him. An exasperated Yama finally offered her three boons if she turned around. 'Ask for anything, except your husband's life.' So Savitri asked a boon for her father-in-law and for her father, and finally asked that she be the mother of Satyavan's children. Yama agreed to all three. Some time later he noticed she was still following him. 'I gave you three boons,' he said. Savitri then said that the third boon of bearing her husband's children could not be fulfilled if Yama took Satyavan's breath to the land of the dead. Yama realized Savitri had outwitted him. To keep his word, he had to restore Satyavan's life.

Savitri's story is narrated in the Mahabharata. Her husband is not chosen for her. She chooses him, despite knowing the risks. She is a determined woman who negotiates with death itself. When given boons, she is generous enough to first think of her father-in-law, then her father and only then of herself. She is also clever enough to outwit the god of death himself. Thus, her power comes from her character and her intelligence, making her a heroine among housewives.

The oldest story of a faithful wife is that of Sukanya, meaning 'a good girl', found in the Aitareya Brahmana and Jaiminiya Brahmana, which are Vedic ritual manuals dated to 800 AD.

Sukanya was a princess who was given in marriage to an old rishi, a sage called Chyavana because she had accidentally blinded him. She served him faithfully. The twin gods of healing, known as Ashwini, found her very beautiful. They sought intimacy with her, but she refused. The gods made her husband as young and handsome as they were and asked her to pick one. Before her were three handsome men, who looked exactly the same. But she noticed that only one of them had feet on the ground, cast a shadow, blinked and perspired. The other two were clearly gods. She chose her human husband, impressing them with her faithfulness.

Is Sukanya driven by love or duty? We can always speculate. That she chooses an old husband over two handsome gods makes her worthy of adoration. Arundhati, the wife of Rishi Vasistha, is another famous sati. Her husband is one of the seven Vedic sages who constitute the Great Bear constellation (Sapta Rishi Mandala). The final star in the constellation is a binary one, naked to the visible eye — embodying the sage Vasistha and his wife, Arundhati, i.e., Mizar and Alcor. Newly-weds are asked to look upon the constellation, so that they will be as faithful to each other as Arundhati was to Vasistha.

The wives of the other six sages of the Great Bear constellation were not as faithful. But their infidelity was involuntary, an accident. They were, without their knowledge, touched by the fire god, Agni, and hence discarded by their husbands. In fury, they moved away and became the six stars of the Pleiades (Krittika) constellation that is part of the Taurus Zodiac. The Krittika goddesses are imagined as wild and dangerous, who can harm mothers and children, unless appeased. The Rishis of the Great Bear constellation are imagined as tranquil and wise, spouting the mantra of the Veda. Sapta Rishi Mandala revolves around the Pole Star in the northern sky, while Pleiades moves along the horizon.

Men's anxiety about their wife's fidelity may have something to do with the paternity of their wife's children. Not letting widows remarry may have something to do with preventing the wife taking her husband's property and his children to her second husband. Rather than using force to shape a wife's behaviour, the narrative of sati ensured women complied voluntarily.

In medieval Sanskrit and Prakrit tales, such as *Sukasaptati*, *Jataka* and *Yashodhara-charitra*, wives of merchants and warriors indulge in adulterous relationships, while their husbands are away for trade or war. Kings return to find their wives with elephant stable keepers; merchants return to find their wives with monks. A faithful wife was an aspiration, a great luck.

Stories of sati were told to encourage women to be faithful to their husbands. This, they were told, would grant them powers to ensure their husbands returned safe from battlefields and perilous journeys abroad. Widowhood was blamed on the woman's character — her inability to ensure his safety. So we find the idea of sati even in 1500-year-old Tamil epics involving mercantile communities, such as *Shilapadikaram*, that was far removed from the Vedic world.

Kannagi pines for her wayward husband, Kovalan, who prefers the company of a courtesan named Madhavi. As long as she is faithful to him, as long as she is true to him, as long as she has desires only for her husband, she has the power of sati. This power ensures that her husband eventually comes back to her. The couple moves to another city in order to restart their life and restore their fortune. But then Kovalan is wrongfully accused of theft and killed by the king of Madurai. Kannagi, in her fury, uses her sati power to set the city of Madurai ablaze. She becomes Goddess Pattini, the chaste wife whose powers can heal and harm.

The Vedic world thrived 3000 years ago. Around 1500 years ago, the Vedic world started being replaced by the world of temples. Stories of enshrined deities were told in the Puranas. Here we finally encounter the famous Hindu trinity of Brahma, Vishnu and

Devdutt Pattanaik

Shiva, who are married to Saraswati, Lakshmi and Durga. Here marriage is the key part of divinity. So is the idea of chastity.

The three goddesses were jealous of Anasuya, Atri's wife, because everyone claimed she was the greatest sati, totally devoted to her husband. So they sent their three husbands to test her chastity. The gods took the form of young hermits. They came to Anasuya's house and said, 'We had taken the vow of renouncing food for twelve years. Twelve years have passed, and to break our fast we need human milk. That is why we come to you.' In other words, the gods wanted Anasuya to breastfeed them. Anasuya had no children, so had no milk in her breasts. But it was improper to turn a guest away unfed. She did not want to doubt the sincerity of the handsome young hermits. Ignoring the ethical and moral dilemma, she offered her breasts to the handsome men, her gaze that of a mother. Such was the integrity of her gaze that the men who sought to suckle her instantly turned into little babies, and Anasuya's breasts began to ooze milk. Those who sought to break Anasuya's vow of chastity, ended up becoming her children. The three goddesses begged Anasuya to let their husbands go. In exchange they gave her three sons: Datta, the wise; Durvasa, the powerful; and Chandra, the handsome moon-god, who fathered the lunar race of kings.

A sati thus has powers over the gods. She can even protect the enemies of gods as we learn in the story of Vrinda, another story found in the Puranas.

Vrinda's husband, Shankhachuda, was an asura, who was so powerful that even Indra, the king of gods, became insecure. He was invincible in war, as he was protected by his wife's chastity. The only way to defeat the asura was to make him vulnerable to weapons. And the only way to do that was to destroy Vrinda's chastity and make her lose her sati powers. Indra achieved this by getting his younger brother, Vishnu, to take the form of Shankhachuda. While the real Shankhachuda was busy fighting Indra, the false Shankhachuda arrived at Vrinda's doorstep. She gazed at her false husband as a true wife. This was enough to take away her sati status. The asura became vulnerable and was killed by Indra, and Vrinda became a widow.

This story introduces a moral and ethical dilemma in the story of a sati. What happens if a demon is protected by her wife's chastity? The good deed of killing a demon demands the bad deed of tricking a woman to be unchaste. Vrinda is equated with Lakshmi, the goddess of wealth, who belongs to victors. The killing of her husband is the killing of her former overlord. War that brings victory and success also creates widows, who curse the victors, before immolating themselves. The immoral nature of war and victory is thus embedded in Vrinda's story.

Vrinda turns into the tulsi plant that is found in the courtyard of every traditional Hindu household, a reminder of the price of even unintentional unfaithfulness. It is said that Vrinda followed Vishnu to his abode in Vaikuntha and stood in his courtyard, demanding to know if she was the chaste wife of Shankhachuda, the asura, or Shankhachuda, the impersonator, i.e. Vishnu. She was a liminal being— located in the courtyard, which was neither outside the house nor inside. She was neither vidhava nor sadhava. She heralded prosperity, but also could not protect her husband. Women who wish to remain sadhava worship this plant every day, at dawn.

Renuka is another sati whose tale presents ethical and moral dilemmas.

Jamadagni's wife, Parashurama's mother, Renuka was so chaste that she could collect water in an unbaked pot. But these powers went away the day she, for a moment, desired another man, a king named Kartaviryarjuna. Because she was no longer a sati, her husband asked their son, Parashurama, to behead his mother with an axe. Later, on Parashurama's request, she was resurrected.

In folk mythology of Karnataka, Parashurama beheads two people, his mother, who is a Brahmin, and another woman, who tries to stop the matricide, a non-Brahmin, a code for someone who does not value the rules of chastity and fidelity. When Renuka is resurrected, the father and son are faced with two women: one with a Brahmin body and one with a Brahmin head. What constitutes the wife: the head or the body?

Jamadagni chooses the one with a Brahmin body. The one with a Brahmin head becomes a goddess, Yellamma, which means 'mother of all'. Yellamma is the earth, the forest, who loves all creatures equally. Renuka is the field, with eyes only for her husband.

In the Tantrik Age (1000 AD to 1500 AD), the chaste wife was equated with celibate holy men (*siddha*) who also had similar magical powers. In the Bhakti Age (1500 AD to 1800 AD), while saints secured similar powers by surrendering to deities in temples, the sati secured her powers by considering her husband as a manifestation of the divine (*pati parmeshwar*).

Shilavati's husband was a gambler, a drunkard, who loved visiting brothels, as a result of which his body was diseased and full of sores. He would force Shilavati to carry him on her shoulders and take him to his gambling den and pleasure houses. Shilavati would dutifully agree. When the gods saw how he treated Shilavati, they were so disgusted that they said that before the sun rose he would die. When Shilavati learnt about this, she forbade the sun from rising so that her husband would not die. Since she was a sati, the sun had no choice but to stay below the horizon. The gods began to panic. The cosmic order was threatened. Everyone begged Shilavati to let go. But Shilavati refused until the gods promised to protect her husband and keep him alive. The gods said her husband would stay alive provided he stayed true to her. The husband agreed, and Shilavati let the sun rise.

Mutual fidelity thus saved a life and a marriage. Shilavati's tale is a good parable—the burden of a good relationship is placed not just on the wife but also on the husband. Reciprocity is propagated. But in most stories, the burden rested with the wife, not the husband. Very rarely do we come across stories of chaste husbands such as Ruru, who negotiates with Yama, god of death, and gives away half his lifespan so that his dead wife, Priyamvada, can be restored to life.

In the Mahabharata, when the Pandavas lose the game of dice and their fortune, they are forced to live in a forest. The sages say that the only one who can rescue them from misery is their wife if she truly loves and cares for them. They proceed to tell the Pandavas the stories of great wives such as Savitri and Damayanti.

Damayanti was a beautiful princess who chose her own husband. She chose the handsome and talented Nala. Unfortunately, for her, Nala had a gambling habit. And one day, he lost all his fortune and was forced to leave his palace. While his children were sent to Damayanti's parental home, Damayanti decided to stand by her husband in this time of crisis. Nala, however, was so ashamed of his failure and misfortune that he decided to abandon Damayanti in her sleep, so that she would be forced to return to her father's house. Damayanti woke up and realized that her husband had run away. She felt sad. Nala did not feel he was worthy of her love. She had more faith in him than he had in himself. After many adventures, after surviving rape attempts and social humiliation, she managed to reach her father's house and set about looking for Nala. She told spies to look for an exceptionally talented but shy man. For none could cook like Nala or ride horses like him or tame elephants like him or identify perfumes like him. Such a man was found, in the kitchen of a king, but he was anything but good-looking. Surely, he could not be Nala. But Damayanti was sure he was Nala, based on the talents of this man. He was hiding from the world, in shame. She had him brought to her father's house. Touched by his wife's love and determination, Nala draped a magical robe that restored his good looks. With his wife's support, he was able to get his fortune back. Life was good once again, all thanks to Damayanti.

In the story of Damayanti, as in the story of Savitri, value is placed not so much on a wife's fidelity as on her love, resilience and support. The concept of sati may have been sold as granting magical powers to faithful wives, but it reveals a yearning of men for a strong wife, one who chooses him, and is true to him and him alone. Not for his wealth, not for his power, but for who he is. She stands by him through thick and thin, in good times and bad. Such a man was truly a fortunate man.

2

Damsels Who Get Bored

*Apsaras are celestial beings, pleasure providers, bound to no man,
and indifferent to matrimony and maternity.*

The Rig Veda tells the story of Urvashi, a celestial woman who abandons her earth-bound husband, Pururava, and seeks the company of her friends, the damsels (*apsara*) of paradise (*swarga*). She ignores her husband's appeal to stay back. She does not seem to care for her children. She is bored and wants to move on. Her nature is that of an apsara, a restless nymph, very different from that of a sati, the chaste wife. Maybe she embodies a female sexuality that existed before, or outside, the Vedic world.

The Vedic world was anchored on chants compiled in the Rig Veda, the oldest Hindu scripture. Put together about 3000 years ago in the Gangetic plains, it contains a thousand hymns praising mostly male gods, composed many centuries earlier, mostly by male poets (*kavi*). Occasionally, in the midst of the chants, we find mention of goddesses, and of women, who yearn for husbands.

- Ghosha and Apala, who have been abandoned by their husbands and who yearn for beauty so that they can get their husbands back.

- Saswati, who seeks the restoration of her husband Asanga's virility.

- Yami, who is sad that her brother, Yama, refuses to be intimate with her, as he does not wish to incur the sin of incest.

- Lopamudra, who seeks the attention of her husband, Agastya, who prefers rituals.

- Indrani, who boasts about the virility of her husband.

- Even the widow is asked to return to the land of the living by grasping the hand of another man.

In this light, Urvashi's rejection of matrimony and motherhood stands out. She seems so unlike other Vedic women that one cannot help but wonder if she belonged to another culture, one that was at odds with the Vedic way.

Around the world, we hear stories of men who fall in love with nymphs and turn them into wives, only to have their heart broken. The nymph stays with her husband only because he has stolen her magical skin (bird feathers in Germany, fish scales in Ireland) and with it her memory. When she eventually finds her skin, her memory is restored, and she returns where she came from. Some folklorists believe this is an Indo–European tale.

Indo–Europeans were Steppe pastoralists from Eurasian regions who introduced horse-drawn spoked-wheel chariot technology to Europe and to India, around 1500 BC, towards the end of the Bronze Age. With them came patriarchy. Urvashi's tale is perhaps the local Indian version of such a tale.

Nymphs in Indo–European mythology were free forces of nature that humans wanted to tame. That is why Greek gods chased nymphs, who turned into plants in order to escape; when caught, they got raped. They perhaps represent a world before patriarchy took deep roots—when women chose lovers, rather than husbands. In patriarchal societies, free women like Urvashi were deemed harlots.

In later literature, male writers are unable to grasp this woman's rejection of her husband and quest for autonomy.

- In the Shatapatha Brahmana, dated to 800 BC, the only reason Urvashi leaves Pururava is because the gods want her back.

- In Kalidasa's play, *Abhigyanashakuntalayam*, dated to 400 AD, the two are separated because of a curse.

In all stories, after Urvashi goes away, Pururava goes mad. His ministers replace him with a worthier, less lovelorn king on the throne.

A similar shift is observed in the story of Shakuntala, the mother of the mighty Bharat, after whom India is named Bharat or the expanse of Bharat.

Dushyant, from the lunar line of kings, was hunting deer in a forest when he encountered a maiden called Shakuntala. She was born from the union of an apsara called Menaka and a hermit called Vishwamitra. A symbol of her triumph and his failure, she was found abandoned on the forest floor and raised by another hermit named Kanva. Dushyant fell in love with her, and they made love before he returned to his palace. He promised he would come back for her. But he never returned.

What happens after that depends on which version of the story you read. This is what the popular version by Kalidasa, composed around 400 AD (1600 years ago), tells us.

When the world finds out that Shakuntala is pregnant, they tell her she should go to her husband's house. But when she reaches the palace, Dushyant does not recognize her. He accuses her of lying, calls her a harlot and kicks her out. We later learn that Dushyant could not remember Shakuntala because of a curse. When the curse is reversed, Dushyant remembers Shakuntala and regrets his harsh words. He looks for her everywhere and finally finds her in the forest. He brings her back to the palace with respect and dignity.

But the story is very different in the earlier Mahabharata version, put down in writing around 100 BC (2000 years ago) but reflects an earlier Vedic age, probably 1000 BC (3000 years ago).

When Shakuntala learnt she was pregnant, she did not crave for Dushyant. She did not want him to be her husband or her child's father. Her father did not ask her about the child's paternity. She delivered the child in the forest and raised him on her own. This went on until one day, when the son asked, 'Who is my father?' In response, Shakuntala took him to Dushyant's palace and introduced father and son. The father refused to acknowledge the son and accused Shakuntala of being a liar and a harlot. Shakuntala clarified that she did not seek matrimony; she simply wanted to introduce her son to his father, about whom he was curious.

The Mahabharata's Shakuntala was like her apsara mother, who did not seek validation from lovers. Unlike her mother, though, she raised her child and felt it was her responsibility to introduce him to his father.

In Atharva Veda, the apsaras are closely connected with the *gandharva*. *Gandha* means something fragrant, complementing *apsa*, which means something fluid, like water and rivers. The two can be linked to flowers: apsara embody the nectar, gandharva embody the fragrance. They embody the sensory and erotic aspect of nature that enables fertility. In later literature, both apsara and gandharva are part of Vasant's entourage, the spring god, who is Kama's companion, the love god. The apsara dances and the gandharva makes music. This is the world of freedom, no bonds or obligation. In the Purana, the apsara and the gandharva are churned out of the ocean of milk, along with Lakshmi, the goddess of fortune, and other objects of pleasure, such as the flowering trees, cosmetics, jewellery, fashion, perfumes.

Apsaras were perhaps originally metaphors for fresh water that came down from the sky as rain, but then rolled away like rivers, towards the sea. No one could control them. Neither Indra, the god of the sky, their lover, nor Varuna, the god of the sea, their father. Later, we learn of gods like Shiva and Vishnu, who control rivers and hence become role models for kings, who control water tanks and canals, much needed for irrigation and creating agricultural wealth. Ganga is caught in the locks of Shiva's hair. Yamuna follows Krishna wherever he goes. When the waters are not around, there is drought and misery. This sterility was later linked to monasticism.

Stories of apsaras became popular with the rise of monastic orders in India, such as Buddhism and Jainism, after 500 BC (2500 years ago). Householders who would invoke Indra and the Vedic gods for fortune, wives and children, started becoming hermits, who rejected all things worldly. These hermits were called *tapasvi*, those who churn inner heat (*tapa*) by practising *tapasya*. Tapa allowed the hermit to break all fetters to the material world. He could break free from the wheel of rebirths (*samadhi*) or acquire occult powers (*siddha*). Either way he became independent of, and more powerful than, Vedic gods.

The apsara is presented as the enemy of hermits. She is weaponized by Vedic gods, who feel threatened when men, instead of invoking them, choose the path of monasticism and the occult. In the Mahabharata, Janapadi seduces Sharadvan. In the Brahma Purana, Pramlocha seduces Kandu. Her role is to draw out the hermit's semen, make him bear children and be part of the material world where they are dependent on the devas who live in swarga. Buddhist Jataka literature also speaks of hermits being seduced by damsels.

A sage called Vibandhaka was seduced by an apsara who took the form of a deer. Thus was born Rishyashringa, with a horn, to remind his father of his failure to control his senses. Rishyashringa was raised without the knowledge of women. But, eventually, he was seduced by damsels. As a result, he lost his magical ability to stop the rain from falling. His sexual awakening ensured rainfall and the dry earth became wet, bursting with green vegetation.

The apsaras do not care about her babies born from her union with the tapasvi. Urvashi abandons her children and leaves them with Pururava. Her sight makes Varuna and Mitra spurt out semen that falls into pots and gives birth to the sages Vasistha and Agastya. Drona is born from the semen spurted out by Bharadvaja into a pot at the sight of an apsara. Suka is born from the semen spurted out by Vyasa on a fire stick at the sight of an apsara who takes the form of a parrot. Menaka abandons her daughter Shakuntala to the mercy of the elements. Janapadi abandons her twins, Kripa and Kripi, on the forest floor.

We can speculate that apsaras probably embody the memories of an ancient time, one before the arrival of patriarchal Aryans, who entered India from Central Asia around 1500 BC. This idea of Aryan immigration into India has been a contentious one. However, we are now confident that a large group of mostly men with a unique Y chromosome entered India roughly 3500 years ago. They came with horses, spoked-wheel chariots and spoke a new language. Similar groups migrated to Iran and Europe, which explains why Indian languages have a lot in common with Persian, and European languages such as Lithuanian and Latin. Our confidence about this migration stems from the new science of ancient DNA analysis that, since 2010, has revolutionized our understanding of human migration around the world. Here is a brief summary of what we know.

- We now know that humans migrated through the Indian subcontinent to South-East Asia over 50,000 years ago from Africa. Our connection with these people is in our use of retroflex sounds (ट, ठ, ड), which are still used in India and found in some communities of Papua New Guinea and Australia. This gene is found all over India.

- Then, around 10,000 years ago, came Iranian farmers that led to wheat and barley farming in north-west India, eventually giving rise to the cities of the Indus Valley and Gujarat coast from 2500 BC (4500 years ago). These cities traded with the Middle East but collapsed following climate change and trade disruptions by 1900 BC (3900 years ago). This gene is also found all over India.

- Then, four centuries after the end of the Harappan civilization, around 1500 BC (about 3500 years ago), two groups of men came into India. Both these groups married local women.

  ※ From the east, via Burma, came speakers of Austroasiatic languages, who brought rice technology. We know very little about them.

  ※ From the west, via Afghanistan, came speakers of Indo–European languages. They identified themselves as Arya and brought the horse-drawn chariot technology. The Aryan male gene is found across much of north India and among elite communities of south India. Men in these regions show lactose tolerance in adults. Adults in rest of India prefer curdled milk.

Was the Aryan immigration violent or non-violent? This is open to interpretation. Those who came to India were mostly men, they married local woman and they wanted to pass on their knowledge, as per Vedic lore, only to sons, not daughters. This indicates they were patriarchal, a practice that probably they introduced to the land.

The Rig Veda was organized and transmitted by men who had Aryan fathers but non-Aryan mothers. These hymns show a yearning of fathers for sons. For this, they needed wives who were faithful to their husbands. The local women probably had very different reproductive practices, not based on fidelity, monogamy and patriarchy. They were apsaras of stories, not satis. This is highly speculative but is suggested by the little information we have from archaeology of the Harappan cities of the Indus Valley and the Gujarat coast that predate the Rig Veda by several centuries.

All information about Harappa come from archaeology, objects, seals and clay figurines found in the ruins of the cities. The Harappan cities are known to be well organized: with thick walls, segregated neighbourhoods and lots of gates. It seems to have been a highly regulated society, where movement was tightly controlled. Even the sanitation and water management systems ensured women did not have to leave the house for ablutions and collecting water. Were the women isolated in courtyards? Harappan cities do seem insular. Despite 700 years of trade with Mesopotamia, we find not a single Mesopotamian seal in India. They even shunned the popular cuneiform script of writing used by their trading partners and preferred their emoji-like writing to manage logistics.

The Harappan women probably invented the rimmed vessels (*lota, handi*) that are still used in kitchens today. They were the first to use masala, especially ginger–garlic paste, and cook brinjal. They were very fond of turbans, like the kind worn by Tibetan and other mountain women even today, and jewellery around the neck, in the ears, on the head and, of course, bangles. The profusion of bangles, made of seashells and camel bones, in these sites reveal that this particular ornament was special to Harappan women, as were beads. Even today, the married or *sumangali* status of women is indicated by bangles (*chuda, chudi*) and beaded chains around the neck (mangalsutra).

There are even suggestions that the Harappan woman used sindoor on their foreheads.

On the few narrative seals we have, we find images of women dancing in groups, being worshipped by men alongside trees and even women stopping two men from fighting. There are seals showing a man taking shelter on a tree, from a tiger that prowls freely on the ground, and other seals that show women as tigers from the waist down, a tiger sphinx, indicating their independent, untamed spirit. The so-called dancing girl of Harappa has bangles in one arm and cowrie shells around her neck. Her stance is of a woman in control. There are no images of couples in Harappa, the kind seen in later Buddhist and Hindu shrines. No images of subservient women. We must be wary of imposing modern patriarchy on ancient Harappan society. It is important to remember that the 'dancing' girl was so named because of the White male gaze of John Marshall, who headed the archaeological department in 1924. He saw in the girl's stance the attitude he had seen in the confident devadasis of India.

We do not know much about Harappan marriage practices. We do know that Harappan people were sea traders, who travelled by boats up and down the Gujarat, Pakistan and Iran coasts. Coastal communities often have matrilineal practices — the woman stays in the mother's house and has many lovers, who are mostly sailors from other lands. The children belong to the mother. The property is inherited by daughters. Anthropologists found this practice in the eastern coast of India, in Kerala and Karnataka, which explains the existence of Jewish, Muslim and Christian communities along the coast. These men from the Middle East were often addressed as Mapillai, Maha-pillai, or special sons, meaning sons-in-law. Maybe this practice existed even during the Bronze Age, when Harappan cities thrived. It may explain why Dholavira has graves without any bodies in them: symbolic graves for lost travellers, who never returned and were presumed dead. In the few cemeteries found in Harappan cities, women were found to be genetically related to each other, but the men were not. At least some sections of Harappan society were matrilineal trading communities.

Vedic hymns describe a world of men. They were composed by male poets for male deities. There are very few female poets and female deities. They include Usha (dawn), Ratri (night), Indrani (wife of Indra),

Aditi (mother of Deva), Prithvi (earth), Saraswati (river), Vak (speech), Aranyani (forest). Most get a single hymn. Usha gets the most: twenty-one out of the 1000 Vedic hymns, but even she is forgotten in later Vedic literature. In fact, by the time of the Purana, dawn is visualized as a male god, Aruna, charioteer of the sun.

Vedic tales are full of childless men seeking children from the gods. They did not mind adopting other people's children. Children abandoned by apsaras were raised by men—Kanva adopted the abandoned Shakuntala; Shantanu adopted Kripa and Kripi. But in time, Vedic men preferred fathering their own sons. They needed wives. The wife additionally granted Vedic men eligibility to access the sacred ritual space and perform the central ritual of yagna. Unmarried men could not perform the yagna. To perform rituals, the Arya needed faithful wives, who sat by their side, adoring them. Not restless nymphs. Satis, not apsaras. Stories of Urvashi capture their alarm. Vedic culture perhaps marks the gradual decline of apsara (matrilineal) practices and gradual adoption of sati (patrilineal) practices. While the mother of the sages Vasistha and Agastya is the apsara Urvashi, their wives, Arundhati and Lopamudra, are satis.

The Mahabharata seems to retain a vague memory of the transition from matrilineal to patrilineal societies.

Brihaspati's wife, Tara, eloped with Chandra, the moon god. Brihaspati was furious and refused to perform the rituals until the gods brought his wife back. Tara returned pregnant. Both Brihaspati and Chandra laid claim to the child in her womb. Tara remained silent. The baby in her womb asked her to tell the world who made her pregnant. She revealed it was Chandra, which made him the biological father. But the gods declared that the child belonged to Brihaspati because he was her lawfully wedded husband.

Thus, we see here a paternity dispute and the decision to make levirate (*niyoga*) legitimate. A woman reduced to a baby-making machine: her child doesn't belong to her but the man who married her. This story draws attention to a very different kind of woman. Tara does not want to be a faithful wife. She will not be forced into loveless marriages. She does not seem to be Vedic. In the Chandogya Upanishad, we find a similar story of paternity.

Jabala's son asks, 'Who is my father?' Jabala replies, 'I do not know. I have been with many men.' Her son goes and tells his teacher that he doesn't know who his father is. All he knows is that his mother is Jabala, and therefore he should be called Jabali, the son of Jabala. The teacher is so impressed by his honesty that he says he shall be known as Satyakam, the one who loves the truth.

Here, there is no moral censure associated with a woman who has many lovers. It is almost as if we are talking about a time where women were not bound to men. It suggests a pre-Vedic world, or a non-Aryan world. It was perhaps the world of autonomy-seeking apsaras who lived in mercantile societies such as the cities of Harappa.

As Indian economy became more agricultural, after 500 AD (1500 years ago), and less mercantile, men travelled less and Vedic patriarchal values became mainstream. But this was resisted by one group of women, who traced their line of descent from apsaras, who rose from the ocean of milk. These were women who were singers, dancers and musicians. Later, they were reviled as courtesans and prostitutes. But they were essentially autonomous women, who did not marry, were unattached to a single man and had lovers instead. They did not own land or trade in goods. They earned their livelihood by providing entertainment and hospitality services to travellers and merchants. This made them very rich. References to these women are found in Buddhist and Jain literature. They served kings, paid taxes, donated orchards to monks and built caves for them. They transmitted their property and their knowledge and skills to their daughters.

Shudraka's play *Mricchakatika* (the little clay cart), composed 2000 years ago, has as its protagonist Vasantsena, a talented and prosperous courtesan, who has lovers and wealth, and everybody desires her almost like the film stars of today. Of course, nowadays, a film star is expected to marry and follow a patriarchal route. These ancient and medieval entertainers were under no such obligations. Jain lore speaks of the talented courtesan Kosha. In Tamil Sangam epics we learn about Madhavi, the courtesan whose mother, Chitrapati, is upset on learning that her granddaughter, Manimekalai, instead of following the family profession, wishes to be a nun. In a 2000-year-old Buddhist scripture, Milindapanna, there is the story of a very successful courtesan called Bindumati who was prosperous even in times of distress.

Bindumati, a courtesan, had the power to reverse the flow of the Ganga. This power came to her, she told King Ashoka, because she treated all her customers as equals. It did not matter if they were priest or warrior or merchant or servant. As long as they paid her fees, she treated them equally. So she was a businesswoman who respected all her customers.

When temple culture rose, these women could maintain their independence only by claiming they were married to the village deity, the *gram deva*, which made them *nagar-vadhu*s (city brides). But there was a time when there was no need for them to be married to God or humans. Theirs was a matrilineal system. Were they carrying forward customs and practices of Harappan times?

In the Mahabharata, Kunti tells Pandu of a time when there was no concept of marriage, and men and women were free to go to each other. However, as the concept of property emerged, men needed to know who their children were so that they could be given their property. This meant they needed women to be faithful to them. This was when the need for chastity arose. Kunti's statement reminds us that the idea of sati came later in Indian society. Before that, women were more apsara, with greater autonomy and agency.

3

Wrapped in Female Flesh

Many a nun refused to adorn their bodies or be limited by the flesh.

Apsara is a woman of paradise linked to many men. Sati is a woman of the household linked to only one man. Then there is the *shramani* or *bhikkuni*, the Jain and Buddhist nun, who is attached to no man. Hindu lore, with its preference for domesticity, has few such women. But they are not entirely absent. One of them is Sulabha, who pays a visit to Janak, in the Mahabharata.

> Sulabha and Janaka were discussing the intellectual aspects of the Vedas. But Sulabha noticed that Janaka was very disturbed during the conversation. Janaka spoke up, 'You are probing my mind like a scholar. I find it uncomfortable because you are a woman.' Sulabha responded, 'I am speaking to you as a scholar, not as a woman. You are supposed to pay attention to my words, to my thoughts, to my ideas. Why are you paying attention to my body? Clearly, you're not evolved enough. Don't you know that, as per Vedanta, all living beings are genderless souls wrapped in gendered bodies? We simply use this gendered body to understand that genderless soul which is our ultimate reality.'

This conversation was recorded 2000 years ago. It also captured the male discomfort with female intellectuals.

About 2500 years ago, in India, Greece and China, following the rise of mercantile practices and use of currency, new philosophical ideas also became popular. In India, it took the form of a hermit revolution. The hermit was called *shraman*, meaning one who strives hard. This effort was not physical but mental. These men sought freedom from all things material — wealth, power, relationships. Liberty in modern times is political and means freedom in society, but the liberation (moksha, *mukti*) sought by shramans was mystical. They sought freedom from society and also freedom from the passions of the body. They abandoned human settlements and searched for solitude in caves. Some even gave up clothes and food. This shramanic revolution started in the region we today call Bihar, on the Gangetic plains east of the Gandak River. This was where the Buddha attainted Buddhahood, where the Jain Tirthankaras were born and where Janaka ruled.

Buddhist monastic order (*sangha*) had monks (*bhikku*) and nuns (*bhikuni*). Jainism also had a community of monks (sadhu) and nuns (*sadhavi*). But the world of hermits was essentially a male domain. Monks were deemed superior to nuns. Nuns could not teach monks. Women were answerable to men. It was said that a nun took thirty years to reach a rank that a man could reach in three years. Buddhism was led by male Buddhas; Jainism was led by Tirthnakara and his *ganadhara*.

There is a gender bias when it comes to male heroes and female heroes in Indian lore. The male hero is typically one who shuns women altogether. The female equivalent was not a nun, but a chaste wife or sati, whose magical powers come from being faithful to a single man. A female ascetic, who had no sexual desires, was treated suspiciously.

The assumption was that a woman's mind and body were far more sensuous than a man's mind and body. That a woman found it harder to control her desires as compared to men. A man's erection could not be hidden but a woman's desires had no obvious physical manifestation and so could be easily hidden.

Male sexuality endowed with the white seed can be controlled by the human mind. In Tantrik texts, female sexuality endowed with the red seed cannot be controlled by the human mind. This is why monks, bearers of the white seed, were believed to be more spiritual, more capable of climbing the spiritual ladder than a nun, who was the bearer of the red seed. Many believed the female body is one generation away from the path of liberation. A nun can earn merit to acquire the male body in her next life and only then walk the final path of liberation.

When the Buddha established his monastic orders, he was not willing to let women become nuns based on his traditional understanding of female sexuality. But when his father died, he noticed his stepmother, Mahaprajapati, weeping. He realized women suffer as much as men. Suffering is not shaped by biology. Since Buddhism is about outgrowing suffering, Buddhism could not be restricted to men, it had to be open to women also. This was how the order of Buddhist nuns came into being. The Buddha is thus shown not just accompanied by a pair of male disciples but also a pair of female disciples, Khema and Uppalavanna.

Khema was King Bimbisara's wife. While her husband was very influenced by Buddhism, she was not. She loved all the beautiful things in life and was not interested in visiting a drab monastery or listening to the spiritual talks of the Buddha. So she never accompanied her husband when he went to meet the Buddha at his monasteries. But knowing that his wife loved beautiful things, the king got his bards to describe the beauty of the monastery to her. This enticed Khema to go to the monastery. She was not drawn to Buddha's speech but to the very beautiful woman who stood beside him. But then, right before her eyes, the beautiful woman transformed into an old, wrinkled hag who collapsed and died. This made Khema realize the impermanence of beautiful things, and she became a nun.

That being said, in his monastic code (*vinaya*), the Buddha listed more rules to discipline the nuns than the monks. There was a reason for this.

Uppalavanna became a nun to avoid disappointing her many suitors. In another tradition, she was a married woman who discovered her husband was having an affair with her own mother, so she abandoned her husband and a newborn daughter and left the city. After many wanderings she married another man. But as the years passed, the man got bored of her and married a younger wife. To Uppalavanna's disgust, the younger wife turned out to be her own daughter, whom she had abandoned long ago. Disturbed by these two events, she abandoned her second husband and chose to become a concubine, unattached to a single man. But even this life did not give her pleasure and, finally, she decided to become a nun of the Buddhist order. Uppalavanna grew in spiritual stature and also developed psychic powers. She used this to take on a male form and escape the male gaze. But, one day, despite her powers, due to bad karma, she could not escape rape. The rapist went to hell. Monks were anxious about Uppalavanna's role in the act, but the Buddha said it was not her fault as she did not give consent. Rules were then formulated to prevent nuns from staying and travelling alone to wild, desolate places.

The Jains tell the story of the arrogant scholar Haribhadra, who realized his limitations when he encountered a Jain nun, Yakini Mahattara. He wanted to be her student, but she directed him to a monk, Jinasena. Haribhadra became the monk's student but acknowledged his debt to the nun by calling himself Yakini-*putra* or the son of the Jain nun.

Devdutt Pattanaik

In Jain lore, the good wife often becomes a nun when the husband becomes a monk. There are many stories where a monk meet his former wife and sexually desires her. To stop her husband from straying, the nun performs the ultimate Jain ritual of *sallekhana*, fasting to death.

Also, in Jain lore, a woman who is tortured by her mother-in-law and husband for serving Jain monks is reborn as a goddess called Ambika. Her chastity causes barren trees to instantly bear fruit and empty wells to immediately fill with water. She is shown holding a baby in her arm. Her husband, full of remorse, kills himself and is reborn as a lion, which becomes her mount. In solitary splendour, Ambika becomes the guardian of Jain monks and sages.

In Jainism, there is a great division between the Digambar, who follow sky-clad (a metaphor for nudity) monks, and the Shwetambar, who follow white-robed monks. These two groups disagree on what Jainism says about the female body. The Digambar believe the female anatomy prevents women from achieving the highest state of omniscience (*kaivalya*). You need a male body for rising into transcendence. The Shwetambar disagree and believe Maru Devi, the mother of the first Tirthankara Rishabhdev, was liberated from her bodily form when she saw her son in the state of omniscience. Consequently, there are many more nuns in the Shwetambar order than in the Digambar order. However, even these nuns are of lesser rank than the monks.

In Digambar lore, the Tirthankara Malli-nath, like all Tirthankaras, had a male body. But in Shvetambar lore, Malli was a woman, a princess.

> Disgusted by the fact that men were willing to fight and kill each other to marry her, Malli called her suitors to her palace and showed them an image that looked exactly like her. The image, however, gave out a terrible odour. It contained the same amount of food that she ate every day in the past month. 'This image does not contain the soul and so her body cannot process the food. My body contains the soul and so it can process the food. Should our life not be a pursuit of that soul, rather than this body and its ephemeral beauty?' she told the men. Malli then gave up the world and became a monk. She rose to the highest rank of Tirthankara.

Malli's female body was the result of Malli's bad karma. In her previous life, she and her friends chose the spiritual path of fasting over the material path of feasting. But she accidentally fasted more than her friends due to illness. She did not inform anyone else about her extra fasts. So while she reaped the rewards of good karma of extra fasting, and would attain the status of Tirthankara, she would do so with a female body, owing to the bad karma of not informing others about her extra efforts. The story captures the discomfort with female bodies in monastic traditions.

We can argue that the obsession with childbirth emerged from a very basic human need of survival at a time of high maternal and infant mortality rate. For a society to survive, more women were needed than men. A tribe's survival depended on its females. The male was generally disposable. In the Puranas, there is the story of Parashurama, who killed all men of the Kshatriya (warriors) clan because they were not noble. But the Kshatriya clan was able to repopulate itself thanks to the survival of one man, who hid in the women's quarters. In other words, for a tribe to survive all the women are needed, but not all the men. Nature privileges the female anatomy over the male anatomy, the egg over the sperm, the red seed over the white seed.

In art, we often find images of seven goddesses with one man (Sapta Matrika with Bhairava). Together they can produce many more children as compared to seven men with one woman (Sapta Rishi with Arundhati). In the creation myths of the Purana, the sage Kashyapa produces all species of living organisms by copulating with different wives.

- Fish through Timi
- Reptiles through Kadru
- Birds through Vinata
- Hooved animals through Surabhi
- Clawed beasts through Surasa

Since all organisms have a common father, it gives rise to the phrase 'Vasudhaiva kutumbakam', or 'the world is one family'. It's a family where children fight over the common inheritance. The world, we are told, owes its existence to a single male. But it needs many females. So a community can afford its men to become hermits, not its women.

A tribe needs mothers not fathers. Hence, the clan always traces its lineage to a mother, the *kula*-devi or clan goddess. By contrast, the gram-deva or village deity is shown to have many wives, belonging to different communities. Khandoba, the folk guardian of Marathas, popular in Deccan regions, has among his wives:

- Banai of the shepherds
- Phulbai of the gardeners
- Rambai of the tailors

- Chandai of the Muslims

In many parts of South Asia, therefore, we find families where only the eldest son is allowed to marry. The younger sons are encouraged to become monks, or they satisfy themselves by going to brothels or sharing the elder brother's wife. This ensures that the family property is not divided.

- In the Himalayan region, only the elder brother marries, and he may share his wife with his brothers, if she is willing.

- In Kerala, the Namboodiri Brahmins only let the eldest son marry and inherit the land.

In both these cases, we realize the importance given to women over men from a reproductive point of view. However, many women refuse to be defined by their bodies, as we learn from this story of Madhavi from the Mahabharata.

It was foretold that Madhavi, Yayati's daughter, would be the mother of four great kings. One day, a sage called Galava visited Yayati and said that he needed 800 horses for his guru, Vishwamitra. Yayati wanted the merit of giving 800 horses to Galava, but he did not have the horses. So, he struck a deal with Galava and said, 'My daughter is capable of bearing four sons, who will become great kings. Take her to four kings, each of whom is willing to give you 200 horses. Let them father her sons.' Galava agreed, and Madhavi was taken across the land and offered to kings, who fathered her sons in exchange for 200 horses. Galava found three such kings. Not finding a fourth king, he gave his guru the 600 horses and the option to father a son with Madhavi, which was worth another 200 horses. When Madhavi returned to her father's house after bearing four sons for four men, Yayati wanted to organize a *swayamvar* ceremony where Madhavi could choose a husband. But Madhavi was so exhausted by her exploitation that she chose to become a nun. Many years later, while she was meditating, her father appeared in a dream and said he had exhausted all the merit he had earned by giving horses to Galava. To continue staying in paradise he needed more merit. Madhavi gave him her merit and asked her sons to give theirs too. At first her sons refused but Madhavi asked them to forgive their grandfather. This is a story of sexual exploitation from the Mahabharata, which will never make it to textbooks or the television.

Hindu lore does narrate stories of nuns, but men are constantly irritated by their presence, as in the case of Sulabha. In Brihadaranyaka Upanishad, Yagnavalkya encounters a nun called Gargi, who asked so many questions that it exasperates him. The Ramayana tells the story of a nun named Swayamprabha, daughter

Devdutt Pattanaik

of Shandili, who is constantly reminded of her female body, despite her pursuit to outgrow it. When a bird flying overhead admired her sexually, it lost its wings and fell to the ground. Its wings were restored only after it apologized. Sexuality follows Kunigarga even after death as per the Mahabharata.

Kunigarga was an old nun who could not enter paradise after death, as she refused to marry. To gain access, she returned to earth, married a young man called Shringavat but spent only one night with him as his wife.

These were women who clearly shunned the traditional roles of wife and mother. But it was never easy.

The battle between male hermits and householders marked the rise of a new form of Hinduism, different from old Vedic rituals. This tension reached its peak around 500 AD (1500 years ago). But then came the Tantrik phase of Hinduism, where sex became a tool to attain magical powers to satisfy the ambitions of kings. This was when caste ideologies thrived, when temples rose, their walls full of sexual and violent imagery. By the fifteenth century (500 years ago), this Tantrik phase was replaced by the more emotional and less sexual Bhakti phase.

- The monastic phase thrived when India witnessed the arrival of many foreign tribes, such as Yavanas (Indo–Greek), Saka (Scythian), Pahalava (Parthian) and Kushan (Yue-Chi) from Central Asia. This was when Buddhism and Jainism thrived, and the old Vedic world waned. Brahmins reimagined themselves through Puranic lore where God was balanced with Goddess, and marriage was seen as a cosmic obligation. If Buddhist dhamma spoke of social withdrawal, Hindu dharma spoke of social engagement. This was an intellectual phase, where the occult and mysticism were not so prominent.

- The Tantrik phase saw a rise of many small political kingdoms across India. It was a world of ambitious warlords who held all the power. So they sought not hermits but magician and sorcerers who could grant them superhuman powers. This was also a shift in art. The walls of monasteries and caves had sexual and violent images of multi-armed and multi-headed supernatural men and women. Occult powers (*siddhi*) obtained through sexual activity was particularly evident in the east: Odisha, Bengal and Himalayan regions. The men proudly proclaimed how they did not spill semen into the woman's bodies; instead they managed to absorb the female fluid squirted at the height of pleasure. Hindus spoke of Bhairava surrounded by yoginis, and Krishna surrounded by *gopika*s. In this phase, there was more conversation on the body and its fluids, rather than the mind. The female yogini was the source of power, to be channelled to the kings, by the male yogi, who was greater than gods.

- The Bhakti phase, which focused more on mind than on body, was amplified after the Muslims arrived. They broke temples and spoke of submission to an all-powerful God. Hindu poet–saints saw the divine as their beloved and sang songs of separation and union. This was the mystical phase of India, where erotic language was used to connect with something supernatural. Here, God did the miracle, not the saint.

From the tenth century onwards, we find stories of men such as Gorakhnath and Matsyendranath across India. These were ascetics whose withdrawal from women gave them magical powers They could walk on water, fly, produce food whenever they wanted and could change their shape and size. They could do so because they avoided the company of women and focused all their energies on spiritual growth. They venerated the mighty Hanuman of the Ramayana, whose power came from celibacy and control over the senses. Yoginis were the enemies of the Nath Yogi. These sensuous women became powerful by seducing celibate men and stripping them of virility. We are told that these yoginis met their match in Nath Yogis, who would exhaust these women sexually and still not release their seed. Here sexual prowess is separated from reproductive functions. A man can satisfy a woman without releasing his semen. This is now called Tantrik sex in some New Age circles. Here there is talk of the womb of the female partner being used as a piston (*vajroli*) to cause the semen to flow in the reverse direction (*urdhva-retas*), up the spine to the brain, causing nodes (*chakra*) to open and reveal secret knowledge and power.

This fascination with sex-magic built on the foundation of celibacy lost its prominence with the arrival of Islam from the twelfth century AD (800 years ago). The Muslims came with two schools of thought—one that valued God's law and the other that valued God's love. The latter school, the Sufi school, had a strong impact on India's own indigenous Bhakti traditions, which began in south India and spread northwards.

The earliest Bhakti poet–saints came from Tamil Nadu: the Nayanar, who venerated Shiva, and the Alvar, who venerated Vishnu. This was observed between the sixth and ninth centuries. Then in the

Karnataka region we find the rise of the Lingayat and Virashaiva movements, based on devotion to Shiva, between the tenth and twelfth centuries. This then becomes the Sant traditions of north India after the fifteenth century. In all these movements, we find women poet–saints appearing in great numbers. They all reject the household and seek solitary refuge in the divine.

Karaikal Ammaiyar was a Nayamnar poet–saint. Her husband was intimidated by the magical powers she had acquired through her devotion. She could feed her husband summer fruits in winter if he so demanded. So he moved out and set up home with another woman. When Karaikal Ammaiyar learnt of this, she was more happy than sad. She was now free from household burdens and free to totally immerse herself in Shiva. She made herself ugly, almost ghoulish, so no man would bother her.

Andal of Tamil Nadu and Meera of Rajasthan were two women of India, separated by almost seven centuries, who wanted to spend all their time adoring the divine, embodied as the charming cowherd Krishna. Andal, who lived in the eighth century AD (1200 years ago), did not want to marry. Meera, who lived in the sixteenth century AD (400 years ago), was in an unhappy marriage and saw widowhood as an escape. Their songs are filled with romance and delight. Perhaps the two women were disappointed by mortal men around them and sought perfection in the divine men of the mythological realm.

Devdutt Pattanaik

4

Demanding Daughters,
Commanding Wives

*The goddess domesticates herself to transform the
hermit into the householder.*

We have heard tales of a man taming the shrew — a wild woman. But in Hindu mythology, a key theme is the story of a woman domesticating a man. However, this is not an act of control; it is an act of empathy and reciprocity. To turn Shiva, the hermit, into Shankara, the householder, the wild Kali becomes the demure Gauri.

The idea of Shiva slowly evolves in later part of the Veda. In the Veda, he is Rudra, a wild and distant and feared deity, with no links to a goddess. The association with Uma, the mountain princess, is found first in the Kena Upanishad, where she introduces him as the embodiment of 'brahman' or the infinite cosmic soul. But she is not his wife. Yet. That idea emerges later, in the Puranic texts, that became the scripture of mainstream Hinduism after the fifth century AD, i.e., fifteen hundred years ago.

The idea of Shiva emerges following the rise of monastic orders in India, 2500 years ago. These monks valorized the outgrowing of hunger through ascetic practices (*tapasya*). The gods who seek food and praise are 'deva' while Shiva, who conquers hunger, is the great god or 'maha-deva'. By making him a householder, Uma showed Shankara the value of empathy. She taught the immortal one to pay attention to mortals, those who have to cope with hunger, fear and rebirth.

In Middle Eastern mythology, God is independent, but humans are dependent. In Hindu mythology, God is the self (me) who engages with the Goddess, who embodies the other (you). In hunger, 'you' are predator, prey or rival, 'you' are 'the other'. Those who outgrow hunger do not distinguish between 'me' and 'you', i.e., the self and the other. They do not pursue domination or control. This sounds very lofty and fancy, but is not very practical.

The Goddess draws attention to regular people, who can venerate Shiva, but still seek food and security. For them, she becomes provider and protector, food and weapons.

- Uma is both Kali (the wild forest) and Gauri (the cultivated field).

- Uma helps Shiva (the hermit) connect with others by becoming Shankara (the householder).

Here the male and the female forms are not to be taken literally. They embody ideas: the male embodies the hungry mind; the female embodies the world around, the food. Just as there is no food without hunger, there is no female without male. So said the ancient Indian storytellers.

This domestication of Shiva countered the Buddhist and the Jain narratives where men became holy when they gave up their households (wife, child, estate, role, responsibility) to become hermits. The reversal was not easy. It involved Uma dying and being reborn.

- She died as Sati and was reborn as Parvati.

- As Sati, she was daughter of a prajapati, a Vedic ritual priest and patriarch; as Parvati, she was a princess, of a patient and understanding mountain king.

- Sati was the 'food' that had been offered but never consumed; Parvati was the one who finally 'fed' the god who was never hungry.

To understand the story of Sati's self-immolation and rebirth as Parvati, we need to appreciate the ritual of yagna, the cornerstone of Vedic society.

- In nature, everyone eats and is eaten. Animals eat the flesh of plants and animals, and their flesh is eaten by other animals and plants. This is visualized in art as Goddess Chamunda, a form of Kali, who is shown feeding on human flesh and bones. Shiva here is visualized as a corpse (*shava*).

- In culture, the point is to feed and be fed. This happens when there is empathy (I pay attention to your hunger) and reciprocity (you pay attention to my hunger). In culture, we turn flesh into food by cooking and serving it, practices that are not seen in nature. This is visualized in art as Goddess Annapurna, a form of Gauri, who is shown in the kitchen feeding everyone, including Shiva, who was called the beggar (*bhikshatan*) then.

In Vedic yagna, the *yajaman* who initiates the ritual invites the devata and feeds the celestial guests and hopes to be fed in return. While feeding he says *svaha*, which means 'this which is mine is now yours'. He hopes the devata will say, *tathastu*, which means 'may your wish be fulfilled'. Today, 3000 years after the yagna was widely practised in the Gangetic plains, Hindus still feed gods (*naivedya*) and hope to be fed by them (prasad). Thus empathy and reciprocity are at the heart of Hindu rituals. The patriarch forgets this and makes all feeding about obligations and duties. The hermit resents this entrapment and chooses freedom—from feeding and from food itself.

Yagna is clearly defined in the Yajur Veda as *dehi ma dadami te* (give me what I give you). This is voluntary exchange: not 'give and take' as in a contract, but 'give to receive'. You earn credit by giving and are in debt by receiving. Creditors and debtors are trapped in the wheel of rebirths, obliged to reclaim and repay debts. Paradise is for creditors; hell is for debtors. To be immortal, one needs to have no debt or credit in your account. Such liberated beings exist in a higher heaven.

- The patriarch Daksha saw the yagna as a tool to control people. His world was full of dependants — gods, ancestors and humans.

  * One was obliged to marry and produce children to repay debts to ancestors (*pitr-hrinn*).

  * One was obliged to provide for Brahmins to repay debts to Vedic sages (*rishi-hrinn*).

  * One was obliged to perform rituals to repay debts to gods (*deva-hrinn*).

- The monks sought liberation, so valued tapasya, in order to burn hunger itself. If they did not consume, they would never be in debt. This would liberate them from all obligations. This was the world of Shiva, the hermit of hermits, the world of independent beings.

- Uma sought to reconcile these two worlds through yoga, based on reciprocity. She wanted Daksha to be generous and write off debts. She wanted Shiva to empathize with the hungers and fears of others. Hers was the world of the dependable ones. In doing so she sought to create a new heaven—where there are no obligations, only love, where the giver is not exploited, and the receiver does not feel entrapped.

In the Purana, Brahma is called the creator. But this is not the creator of nature, as in Middle Eastern mythologies. He is the creator of culture—all things man-made. Brahma's culture is based on yagna. Rishi institutes the Vedic practices. Prajapati maintains it. Shiva is the destroyer, as he rejects the control of culture (dharma) and values the freedom of nature (moksha).

Daksha (whose name means skilled) was a great prajapati. His daughters were his offerings (svaha) to gods. But one of his offerings wanted to choose the recipient. This was his youngest daughter, Sati. She refused to be passive food; she wanted to be the active feeder. She did not let her father choose her groom; she wanted to choose her groom. She wanted agency. She did not want to be chattel. Worse, Sati chose Shiva as her groom. Daksha despised Shiva as he had rejected the idea of the yagna. He did not feed. He did not want to be fed. He sought to overcome hunger. He wandered aimlessly, in the company of ghosts and dogs, matting his hair, smearing his limbs with ash, wrapping his body with animal hide. Daksha did not give Sati permission to marry Shiva. A defiant Sati declared herself to be Shiva's wife and walked out of her father's house. To teach his daughter a lesson, Daksha conducted a yagna and invited all his sons-in-law for the ceremony. Everyone except Shiva and Sati. Shiva did not mind or care. But Sati was upset. She decided she would go uninvited to her father's house. She wanted Shiva to come with her but Shiva did not care. When she arrived, her father did not welcome her as his daughter but insulted her as the wife of a man he despised, a man who did not feed anyone, did not bother to comfort anyone, one who was uncouth, impure and preferred the inauspicious dominion of wild beasts, wild plants and ghosts. Sati tried to explain the hermit ideology to her father, that Shiva was Maha-deva (the great God), so called because he was greater than deva (God). The devas were hungry and needed to be fed, but Shiva had overcome hunger and hence did not eat, had no debts, was free, unafraid of death and liberated from the obligations of life. Thus he was greater than the ancestors who were trapped in the wheel of rebirths. But then Sati realized what her father had said was also true. Her husband did not care for other people's hunger. He fed no one. He was under no obligation. He had no compassion either. He was the indifferent one (*udasin*). She was trapped between a dominant father and an apathetic husband. A father who did not care for her needs and a husband who did not see her needs. As a result, she decided to leap into the ritual fire of her father's yagna and kill herself. The fire refused to burn her, so she invoked her inner fire and burnt herself.

This is among the oldest stories of the Goddess, emerging 1500 years ago, when the earliest images of both Chamunda and Annapurna appeared on temple walls. Why did Sati leap into the ritual fire? Nothing in mythological tales is accidental. Fire is the mouth of gods. The gods are fed through fire. By jumping into the sacred fire lit by her father, Sati made herself the food being offered to Shiva. Who was offering this food? Was it Sati herself? Or Daksha, the official yajaman?

Devdutt Pattanaik

Sati's self-immolation and righteous indignation has been turned into the story of the 'model wife' in popular storytelling. It is conflated with the historical practice of widows burning themselves on their husband's funeral pyre, so that no one could abuse the wife's living body to insult the dead husband's memory. The Vedic symbolism is totally lost as popular lore does not place the story in history—a period when the Vedic householder was pushing back against the doctrine of hermits. The story marks the beginning of a new, reimagined Hinduism that would no longer ignore the feminine.

The old Vedic ways were focused on male gods. The monastic orders were forced on male ascetics. In the Vedic world, women were objects of pleasure. In the monastic world, women were objects of temptations. Women were not seen as agents. The old Vedic ways focused on the ritual obligation (dharma). It ignored the underlying emotion. The hermits rejected this obligation and sought freedom (moksha). Both overlooked that the primal purpose of the ritual was to enable empathy and reciprocity. To remind everyone of this underlying purpose, the female form was re-invoked, through the tale of Sati.

The tension between the patriarch and the hermit shapes Sati's story. In it, we find a woman trapped between two extreme ways of thinking. On one side is a highly regulated culture where everyone is bound to duty. On the other is the indifferent world of nature where no one cares for anybody. The patriarch wants obedient daughters and faithful wives. The hermit seeks nothing and so values nothing, neither daughter nor wife. The patriarch controls everyone through food; the hermit gives up food. In Daksha's world, Sati is controlled; in Shiva's world, Sati does not matter. Torn between these two worlds, Sati decides to kill herself, hoping her death will force transformation.

When the news of Sati's death reached Shiva, something unpredictable happened. The indifferent one became sensitive and reacted! The cold icy mountain exploded like a volcano. He suddenly felt her loss, her pain, her sorrow, her disappointment. The yagna that was designed to feed the hungry had consumed her. And no one cared, neither her father nor her husband. Shiva transformed into a fierce being, filled with outrage. His eyes turned red, his teeth turned into fangs, his fingers into claws. He becomes Virabhadra. He rushed into the ritual precinct of Daksha and proceeded to destroy the altar. He was disgusted by the sight of Daksha continuing to perform the ritual even after his daughter's death, as if nothing had happened. His army of ghost and ghouls contaminated the sacred precinct, smashed the pots, ripped the tapestries, polluted the offerings with vile blood, pus and urine,

Devdutt Pattanaik

filled the air with howls and screams, and rendered everything inauspicious. Virabhadra–Shiva then raised his sword and beheaded Daksha. The devas, who had assembled for the yagna, begged Shiva to stop. They told Shiva that unless the yagna was complete, nobody would feed them. If nobody fed them, how would they feed the rest of the world? The whole world would cease to exist. There would be no rainfall, food would not grow, plants would wither, animals would starve. The world existed because of food. In nature, the predator fed on its prey, the eater was eaten. In culture, humans fed each other. Life was about food and food was about life. We fed and were fed. We ate and we were eaten. No yagna, no food, no life. Listening to these words, Shiva calmed down and decided to resurrect Daksha, replacing his cut head with that of a goat. He then found Sati's body lying in the fire altar. He picked it up. For a long time, Shiva clung to the corpse and wandered the earth, endlessly howling. Shiva's sorrow was unbearable. So the gods got Vishnu to cut Sati's corpse into tiny pieces. These fell on earth and became centres of Goddess worship, the first temples.

Was Sati's body food to be cooked? Was her flesh food? Was her body an offering for Shiva? Was her body a corpse being cremated? Did Sati turn the three auspicious, life-giving Vedic fires into one inauspicious, death-accepting funeral pyre, until Shiva pulled her body out and carried it on his shoulder?

Parts of the body fell in different parts of India where temples were established, temples of fertility visited by householders and housewives even today. These were perhaps pre-Vedic shrines visited and worshipped by tribes who venerated nature as the goddess. By acknowledging these shrines, or seats (*peetha*) as portions of Sati's flesh, the new Hindu order was seeking to overshadow shrines, or reliquaries (*stupa*) where bones of the Buddha were being worshipped. These newly mainstreamed centres of worship were about participating in life, feeding and being fed. Buddhist shrines were about controlling hunger and rising above suffering and joy.

With Sati's body gone, Shiva was able to think again. He retired to the mountain and decided he would never feel again. Sati had forced him to feel pain, suffering and anger. If there had been no Sati in his life, he would have never felt pain, suffering and anger. And thus, he decided to isolate himself and be a hermit once again, in full control over his senses and mind.

But Sati had not given up on Shiva. She took birth as Parvati, daughter of the mountains. This is the first explicit story of rebirth in the Puranic tradition. The old Vedic scriptures do not overtly refer to rebirth; it is implied at best.

The word Parvati comes from the word *parvat*, which means mountain. She was the daughter of Himavan, the king of the mountains. Parvati was determined to make Shiva her husband. In her previous life Sati had left her father's house, broken relations with him and forced Shiva to marry her. In this life her approach was different. She asked her father's permission to marry Shiva.

Himavan asked Parvati how she would convince a hermit to be her husband? Parvati responded by becoming an ascetic herself. She wrapped herself in bark, smeared her body with ash and sat in front of Shiva to meditate. She controlled her senses, her mind, her heart and withdrew inwards. She overpowered her desires, her hungers. So powerful was her meditation that Shiva was drawn towards her. 'What do you want?' Shiva asked Parvati. Parvati replied, 'The same thing that you want. Nothing. I want to desire nothing. I want to be like you, hungry for nothing. When we have no desires, when we have no hunger, we will never be disappointed or frustrated. Our heart will not break, we will never be angry or jealous or greedy. We will be at peace with the world. Isn't that what you are practising? I want to practise the same thing.' Parvati continued, 'You are surrounded by ghosts. They are hungry for life. Only if they are reborn can they be hermits and control hunger like you. But if everyone is a hermit, how will ghosts be reborn? The dead are hungry for life. The immortal gods are hungry for praise and offerings. Every living being is hungry for something. Only you, Maha-deva, is hungry for nothing. The dead cannot feed anyone, the devas feed no one unless they are fed, and even you, Maha-deva, are uninterested in the hungry. Who feeds the hungry then? When I see the hungry, I wish to feed them, be the food that takes away hunger. Can you, who do not eat, provide food for the hungry? You, who seek no wife, can you be my husband? You who have conquered your hunger, can you spare a thought for other people's hunger.'

As Parvati spoke, Shiva realized that the ascetic path, the path of a hermit, was self-serving, it benefitted no one. When it destroyed hunger, it took away the need for food, for life itself. He recalled the words of the devas: 'All life is food, all living is feeding.' In nature, we seek food as no one feeds us. In culture, someone feeds us. If there is no hunger, there is no need for culture or nature. There is no food, no one to feed, no one who feeds. Shiva realized that the hermit Parvati who was sitting in front of his cave was helping him appreciate the importance of food and desire. Hunger exists for a reason. Food exists for a reason. A world without desire is a world where nothing has value.

'I don't want wife or children. So how can I be a husband or a father?' asked Shiva. Parvati replied, 'The first step is for you to come to my father's house like a groom and ask for my hand in marriage. In my last life, as Sati, I walked away from my father's house and forced you to be my husband. But in this life, I want you to come to my father's house and ask for my hand in marriage. I want my father to give me away. Sati did not think of the other. Daksha did not think of the other. The old Shiva did not think of the other. But the new Shiva has to think of the other. Parvati will think of the other. Let us think about my father, my mother, and how they respond to your proposal.' So Shiva arrived at Parvati's doorstep as a groom. But he did not know how to be a groom. Instead of clothes, he wore animal hide. Instead of cosmetics, he had ash on his skin. Instead of garlands, he had snakes around his neck. Instead of a mare, he had a bull.

His family was made of ghosts. He came drinking poison and smoking narcotics. The sight of such a groom horrified Parvati's parents. They refused to give Shiva their daughter. 'He cannot take care of himself. How can he take care of you?' they said. To this Parvati responded, 'I can take care of him. He does not have to take care of me.' To this, Himavan had no response. Seeing that Parvati was willing to give up her life as a princess for him, Shiva decided to make an effort too. With the help of the deva, he made himself presentable at the wedding altar. He was bathed, wrapped in fine fabric, anointed with fragrance, adorned with jewellery and bedecked with flowers. A great wedding was celebrated. Shiva became the husband, Shankara, and Parvati became the wife, Uma. Together they decided to set up home atop Mount Kailasa.

In the absence of Uma, Shiva is visualized as a formless aniconic rock, the Linga stone. With her, the formless rock gives way to various forms:

- Uma-pati, the husband of Uma, who tells her stories and answers her questions.

- Veena-dhari, who plays the lute, inspired by Uma.

- Nataraja, who dances, inspired by Uma.

- Vrishabha-natha, the wild bull whose virility makes the earth fertile.

- Pinaka-dhari, who shoots arrows and protects gods from asuras.

- Kailasa-pati, who protects his mountain from being uprooted by demons like Ravana.

- Bhikshatana, the beggar who receives food for his followers, from the kitchen of Uma.

- Dakshina-murti, who faces the south, the land of the dead, and comforts the ancestors.

- Andhaka-natha, who destroys the demon of darkness and protects his wife.

- Gajantaka, who flays alive the elephant of lust, but uses its head to resurrect Parvati's son.

- Ganga-dhara, from whose locks flow Ganga, enabling the dead to be reborn.

The rebirth of Sati, and the marriage of Shiva and Parvati, are the two events that enabled the transformation of the hermit into a householder. Before this story was told, the dominant story was that of the Buddhist and Jain hermit who challenged the ritual ways of the Vedic patriarch. The transformation included new ideas not found in Vedic lore — the idea of rebirth and the idea of the other. The self is *jiva* while the other is *para*. Every organism has to deal with infinite other beings, i.e., *param*. Most live isolated lives, disconnected (*viyoga*) from others, feeling lost and trapped. However, union (yoga) with the other (para) and with infinite others (param) results in connection and leads to the expansion (*brah-*) of the mind (*mana*) and grants liberation (moksha) to the self (jiva). This subtle and complex metaphysics becomes accessible to farmers, boatmen, traders, warriors, priests, herdsmen, fishermen, and entertainers of India through story and art.

For the first time in Indian art, from the fifth century onwards, 1500 years ago, we find images of Uma–Maheshwara, with the wife seated on the husband's lap, both at the same eye level, her arms on his shoulder, his arms wrapped around her waist, smiling at each other. This intimate portrait is in direct contrast to the serene, meditative stances of the Buddha and the Jina; thus the female asserted her presence. Together, this couple produces two sons, who offer the world what it needs:

- Kartikeya, the mighty, protects the insecure world and also evokes restraint.

- Ganesha, the elephant-headed, provides food with prosperity and also evokes contentment.

Shiva thus becomes a householder. This was the Puranic householder, very different from the earlier Vedic householder.

- The Vedic householder was the patriarch, the *grihapati*, who fed the other and invested in others, entrapping them in a web of debts and obligations, creating an ecosystem of dependants. This was the world that Sati walked away from.

- The Puranic householder was the *grihastha*, one who fed the other, to satisfy the other's hunger, while pursuing contentment for the self. This was the world into which Parvati entered.

In the household of Uma–Maheshwara, the other took precedence over the self: the husband who thought about the wife, the wife who thought about the husband, the parent who thought about the child, the child who thought about the parent. A household where everybody thought about each other.

5

Autonomous Homemakers

The goddess battles for autonomy, food and security.

Traditionally, a Shiva temple had no images. But there were a lot of symbols. There is an aniconic pillar-shaped rock called Shiva-linga, which literally means the symbol of Shiva. This is described by many non-Hindu art historians as the phallus, a metaphor that is often taken literally, much to the irritation of the puritan.

The aniconic pillar sometimes has a square base, which then becomes octagonal and finally cylindrical, a symbolic journey from the finite to the infinite, from the fixed to the fluid, from culture to nature. The pillar stands on a trough, the yoni-patta, identified as the Goddess. The devotee who visits the temple cannot circumambulate the Shiva-linga; the path is blocked by the yoni-patta, which stretches towards the northern direction, a reminder to all that God is incomplete without the Goddess. The trough gives the aniconic stone an orientation by pointing to the north, and identifying itself as being on the left side of the deity. The following story from south Indian temple lore explains why Shiva himself does not want anyone to go around him.

When Bhringi tried to go around Shiva, he was told to go around Uma too. Bhringi refused, and tried going in between them. So Shiva merged his body with Uma's. Bhringi took the form of a bee and tried to bore a path between the two halves. Furious,

Bhringi was stripped of the flesh and blood of his body, tissues that come from the mother. Reduced to bones, he could not stand up. He realized the complementary nature of flesh and bones, female and male, matter and mind.

In Hindu mythology, Uma has many forms:

- The wild Kali, of the forest
- The domestic Gauri, of the field
- The fearsome Chamunda, of the crematorium
- The powerful Durga, of the battlefield
- The affectionate Annapurna, of the kitchen

Uma is not forced to take these forms. She chooses them. She protects and provides for her family, as her guileless wild husband is clueless about household responsibilities. She accepts his ignorance and guileless nature. In temples, she is visualized as Durga, bedecked as bride, but performing the role of a warrior, battling demons, with hair unbound, indicating her freedom. Her devotees argue if she is superior to Shiva, but she has no urge for superiority. She is what she is. Without him, she has no family. Without her, he is alone, without meaning.

The Goddess is always autonomous. She is never controlled by male gods. She chooses her role as wife, daughter, mother, protector and provider. She does not see herself superior, or inferior, to her male counterpart. The understanding of freedom and equality is very different from the one we find in other cultures.

- In Middle Eastern mythology, freedom is liberation of slaves from Egypt, return of exiles from Babylon, defeat of the devil, who draws Adam and Eve out of Eden. God's people are equally bound by God's law.

- In Greek mythology, a hero seeks freedom from the machinations of the Olympians and the Fates. Everyone knows the Olympians have favourites, and so there is no equality in this world.

- In India, the hermit seeks freedom from sensory temptations. When free, he appreciates the equality of all beings as being driven by hunger and fear.

It is important to keep the cultural context in mind while appreciating gender roles in India. Many people tend to globalize Western ideas. The assumption is that Western thought is rational, hence universal. It is not. It is deeply influenced by Greek individualism and Middle Eastern collectivism, where male characters clearly dominate women.

- In Greek mythology, the story of creation illustrates how the gods gradually overshadowed the goddesses. The sky God, Uranus, choked the earth Goddess, Gaia. The time when God Cronus ate the children of the season Goddess, Rhea. Zeus, the king of Olympus, cheated on Hera, the Goddess of the household, and fathered many gods and heroes with reluctant goddesses, nymphs and mortals.

- In the Jewish Bible, women are answerable to men because Eve, the first woman, succumbed to the devil, broke God's commandment, ate the fruit of the forbidden tree and goaded Adam, the first man, to do the same. In the Christian Bible, God produced his son with a virgin woman. In the Quran, in the conversation between Allah and his final prophet, goddesses are deemed false gods and their worship is forbidden. Those who obey God unconditionally (*halal*) will go to heaven (*jannat*). God in monotheism is avowedly male.

When the West renounced religion and declared itself atheist, it saw the world in an eternal state of unresolved conflict between various classes and genders. It was apparent that women, like the lower classes, were denied wealth and power. They were treated by men just as Greek gods treated goddesses and nymphs, and as the God of monotheism punished the daughters of Eve. Such overt patriarchy is missing in Indian mythology.

- In Buddhist lore, the Buddha shuns the material world that is associated with women. But he is often dependent on women, such as Sujata, who feed him. In later Buddhism, the female Tara embodies wisdom. She complements the Buddha, who embodies compassion. In Tantrik Buddhism, the female biology plays an important role in enabling the male biology attain supernatural powers through occult practices known as siddha.

- In Jain lore, the Tirthankara, like the Buddha, shun the material world, assumed to be anchored by mothers, wives, sisters and daughters. There are goddesses who guard these sages, known as yakshis, who, like all pious women, will eventually gain male bodies and be liberated from the material world.

- In Hindu lore, the idea of God is incomplete without the Goddess. Shiva becomes half a woman by embracing Shakti. Vishnu transforms into the enchantress Mohini to preserve order. Brahma and his son Daksha are beheaded in tales where they are shown chasing or controlling their daughters.

In folk narratives, the mother-goddess created the Hindu trinity.

Adi–Maya–Shakti (primal–delusion–power) wanted a partner, a lover, a husband. But Brahma addressed her as 'mother' and Vishnu as 'sister'. So she chose Shiva, who had remained silent. Shiva agreed to be her lover provided she gave him her third eye as a gift. She gave it to him. He used it to reduce her to a pile of ash. He divided it into three parts from which emerged Saraswati, who went to Brahma, Lakshmi, who went to Vishnu, and Kali, who went to Shiva. Saraswati was knowledge who would enlighten the ignorant Brahma; Vishnu was the perfect steward for the resources embodied in Lakshmi; and Kali was the force who alone could awaken the withdrawn Shiva.

Genders are used here as metaphors to communicate ideas. There is ambiguity about who created whom: Did God create the Goddess or did the Goddess create God? The mainstream Rig Veda reflects this folk idea through the line, 'The father creates the mother and the mother creates the father.'

There is a tendency among Western academicians to isolate the wild Kali, who dances on top of Shiva's chest, from other forms of the Goddess. But the Goddess is part of a spectrum — the other end manifesting as the domesticated Gauri, who was devoted to her household. No one forced Kali to become Gauri. She transformed to transform him. Culture is not just a function of domesticating the forest (the Goddess), it is also a function of elevating the mind (the God). God, in Hinduism, is not the patriarch out there; God is the mind within all of us.

- Brahma embodies the ego, who seeks to control the Goddess and so is deemed unworthy of worship.

- Shiva is the hermit who, under the influence of the Goddess, becomes a householder and so is worshipped.

- Vishnu is the enlightened householder who protects the Goddess, who nourishes the world. When Vishnu sleeps, the Goddess takes over the role of protection and fights demons.

Liberty in Western thought is freedom in society, from social norms, enabled by the state. Liberty in Indian thought is freedom from society, from social norms, physically for the hermit and psychologically for the householder. Thus, in Indian mythology all conversations of freedom take two forms:

- In monastic traditions, the hermit shuns the feminine, and makes the journey towards nothingness (*shunya*), the end of identity itself.

- In householder traditions, the man and the woman respect each other's autonomy as expressed through tales of Shiva and Uma, Vishnu and Lakshmi, Brahma and Saraswati. Here freedom comes from union (yoga) and embracing the infinite (*ananta*).

Durga does not reject men. She enables men. She gets Shiva to pay her attention. Her children provide qualities (restraint of the invincible Kartikeya, contentment of the unstoppable Ganesha) that will enable humans to have good relationships.

When did the Goddess appear in Indian thought? This is a mystery.

In 10,000-year-old Stone Age cave paintings from India, we find images of men hunting and women taking care of children or weaving baskets. There is division of labour but no hierarchy.

There are many clay images of bejewelled women in 4500-year-old Harappan cities. There are also images of women in seals of this ancient mercantile civilization that thrived for seven centuries in the Indus Valley Civilization and traded with the Middle

East. But there are no images of dominating men or domesticated couples. Instead we have:

- A woman emerging from a tree, being worshipped by a man.

- A group of women dancing in a group.

- A woman with bangles stopping two men from fighting.

- A woman becoming half a tiger.

- A woman with horns battling.

The 3000-year-old Vedas reveal a world dominated by gods: Indra (sky-god, solar hero), Agni (fire), Soma (heat-generating vegetation that is eventually identified with the moon). There are very few goddesses, who embody motherhood (Aditi), the earth (Prithvi), the forest (Aranyani) and the dawn (Usha). Here we find two layers of hymns:

- The first layer divides the year into two parts: the warm half of the year controlled by gods (deva) and the cold half of the year controlled by ancestors (pitr). This reveals a time when the Aryas were still north of the Himalayas, migrating northwards in summer and southwards in winter, with their cattle.

- The second layer divides the year into three parts: monsoon, pre-monsoon summer, post-monsoon winter. This reveals a time when the Aryas were south of the Himalayas, experiencing the four months of monsoon rains. The nomadic people became more sedentary. Cattle herders gradually became farmers.

During the four months of rains, known as Chaturmaas, the cows refused to move on wet slippery earth, and the pastoral people were forced to stay in one place, protecting their fires from the rains. They came to believe that during the rains, the gods went to sleep, and the world was full of demons and the spirits of ancestors. They sought protection. It is in this period of four months that goddess stories were told by the natives.

A shape-shifting demon had acquired so much power that no single god could defeat him. So the gods came together, released their individual powers and merged it into a collective force. This took the form of a woman called Durga, who held the weapons of all the gods in her many hands. Durga rode into battle on a lion and defeated the shape-shifting demon, beheading him when he took the form of a buffalo, the creature who loves water. This violence resulted in security. This violence also resulted in prosperity. The victory of the Goddess happened just as the rainy season drew to a close, the sky was clear with the bright autumn moon, and the earth was green, ready for harvest.

The violence of Durga, her killing of the buffalo-demon, is a reminder of the essential role of violence in life.

- Violence protects the prey from predators.

- Violence nourishes the predator by turning prey into food.

It is violence that transforms nature into culture. Forests have to be burnt to clear land for villages and fields. Trees have to be cut to produce wood. Bulls have to be castrated to turn them into oxen who can pull the plough and the cart. Pests have to be killed to protect the crop. The very act of cooking involves violence: the threshing of grain, the pounding of flour, the chopping, the steaming, the roasting, the grinding, the frying and the boiling. The transformation of the wild Kali into the domestic, cultivated Gauri is itself a violent act, one that ends her autonomy but nourishes the household.

That is why the Goddess has always existed in the imagination of the commonfolk in many forms:

- Vana-Chandi was the wild forest with hair unbound.

- Rana-Chandi was the warrior goddess, who fed on the flesh of fallen warriors. This was the liminal space between nature and culture, where humans behaved like animals, killed each other, and established borders and hierarchies.

- Mangala-Chandi was the goddess of the household, helping women cope with insecurities of life, loneliness, trauma, hunger, abuse, absence of parents, spouses, children and siblings.

- Jari-Mari, the goddess of fevers, miscarriages, epidemics and droughts, a form the goddess took when she was angry and upset.

Into this indigenous world of the Goddess came Vedic ideas. This gave rise to a new, reimagined Hinduism of the Puranas, that became visible after 500 AD on cave and temple walls. New stories were told of how God engaged with the Goddess.

- The Goddess refused to be controlled by Brahma, who sought to domesticate her.

- She chose to be wife of the independent Shiva and make him part of culture.

- She was wooed by the dependable Vishnu, for he knows that all wealth and power and knowledge come from her.

Humans have to strive to be less than the needy, controlling Brahma, more like the independent Shiva and dependable Vishnu. The Goddess was not an object; she was an agent.

Many kings in India and South-East Asia identified themselves with Shiva and Vishnu. For only by emulating the independent Shiva and the dependable Vishnu could they transform nature into culture and establish prosperous kingdoms. This kingdom was visualized as the Goddess in her domesticated form.

Across India, every village is visualized as a goddess. Every kingdom is visualized as a goddess. Lion-riding, buffalo-killing Durga became the goddess of kings. She bestows kingship upon the worthy. The worthy are supposed to create an ecosystem which is safe and provides opportunity for the generation of wealth, which can be used to generate knowledge. To remind kings of their duty, in spring and in autumn, before and after the rains, kings were told to worship Durga along with her children:

- Lakshmi, goddess of abundance
- Saraswati, goddess of arts
- Kartikeya, god who secures and protects

- Ganesha, god who removes obstacles and provides satisfaction

There are many stories where kings are warned not to abuse their power, exploit the land they are supposed to govern. Here is a story from the mountain kingdom of Nepal.

> Every evening when the palace slept, the Goddess would come to play dice with the king. They would have fun all night. During the course of the game, the Goddess would advise the king on matters of state. Over time, the king started to desire the goddess. The Goddess noticed the lust in his eyes. She disappeared and refused to play dice with him. Soon, the king's fortunes waned. He found himself surrounded by enemies inside the palace and outside in battle. His land suffered droughts, epidemics and major calamities. He apologized to the Goddess. He swore, he would look upon her, and his kingdom, as a father looks upon his child, not as a predator looks upon a prey.

A similar story is found in Gujarat, located thousands of miles to the west of Nepal, near the sea.

> A goddess who lived atop mountains loved to come down and dance with their devotees on full-moon nights. A local king saw her, tried to woo her and would not take no for an answer. Enraged, she

terrified him with her fierce form—riding lions, bearing weapons in multiple arms, adorning herself with the limbs, entrails and heads of men who bothered her and drinking their blood with relish. She threatened to take away his kingship until he apologized and established festivals and fairs in her honour.

Such stories are a reminder of what is expected of kings. They exist to protect and provide for the kingdom. The kingdom does not exist to protect and provide for them. To remind them of this, during festivals little girls are worshipped as the Goddess.

During rituals, everyone is reminded of how the Goddess was created, by the union of powers of many gods. Everyone provides something for the worship—the farmers provide the straw, the herders provide the leather and the milk, the potter brings the clay, the weaver offers the cloth, the gardener offers garlands, the hunter offers meat, the farmer brings vegetables, the carpenter brings the wood. A kingdom thrives when its constituent parts work together as an organism, when parts serve the whole, and the whole serves the part. As we integrate, as the part engages with other parts, freedom emerges not from isolation and indifference, but from mutual respect.

One cannot help but wonder if the relationship of a king and his kingdom captured the way the sages expected husbands to behave with their wives. Together the couple created the household. She was Durga, the protector, and Annapurna, the provider. He had to be Shiva, who listens to her, and Vishnu, who looks out for her. Both were autonomous. Neither controlled the other. Neither was superior or inferior, master or servant. Both gave meaning to each other: two equal parts of a single whole.

Devdutt Pattanaik

6

Wooing Fickle Fortune

Fortune was first embodied as a goddess by Buddhists, seated in a lotus pond, surrounded by elephants.

Today's politicians keep referring to themselves as obedient children of Bharat Mata or Mother India, who seek to liberate her. But in medieval India, kings referred to themselves as Lakshmi-vallaha, the beloved of fortune. This goddess of fortune was fickle. If the king failed to protect her or keep her happy, she ran away, into the arms of a worthier man, a better ruler. This was why she was called Chanchala, the restless one, the one who has to be wooed, the one who cannot be taken for granted.

In Hindu mythology, Lakshmi exists in two places:

- Swarga, the abode of Indra, which was full of dancers and musicians. Lakshmi was unhappy here and kept threatening to leave, making Indra eternally insecure. No one worships Indra any more, as they did in Vedic times.

- Vaikuntha, the abode of Vishnu. Lakshmi was happy here and kept coming back, voluntarily. Hence, Vaikuntha was described as the ocean of milk, or as Go-loka, the abode of the celestial cow. Grand temples are built for Vishnu, where he is shown enjoying life, listening to music, enjoying banquets, wearing fine clothes, adorning himself with flowers, jewellery and perfumes, reclining on his bed, riding on boats, chariots, palanquins or playing on the swing.

Indra and Vishnu see Lakshmi differently:

- Indra sees what Lakshmi can do for him.
- Vishnu sees what he can do for Lakshmi.

Vishnu knows that Lakshmi takes away hunger. That is what makes Lakshmi meaningful and venerable. She embodies the plants and animals that the hungry consume. But human hunger is greater. Our hunger makes us seek comfort — clothes, housing, transport, entertainment. We are hungry for security, so we cling to Lakshmi, do not let her go, hoard her to satisfy our future hungers. But Lakshmi cannot take away insecurity. If anything, she ends up amplifying insecurity and making us hungrier, driving us mad with craving. That is why humans hoard.

Additionally, humans seek meaning. We wonder who we are. What is our purpose? Why do we exist? All plants and animals exist to feed other plants and animals. But humans want to believe they have a higher purpose. We cannot possibly be just food, like Lakshmi, meant to nourish others. So we give ourselves meaning by turning Lakshmi into property.

- We start believing we are who we have.
- We are greater if we have more Lakshmi. We are lesser if we have less Lakshmi.

So food is not just to be consumed for comfort, or hoarded for security; it has to be cornered, denied to others, in order to control and dominate others, so as to feel important, valued and meaningful.

In Indra stories we see how Lakshmi is misunderstood. In Vishnu stories we see how Lakshmi can be understood. A study of Lakshmi's stories, and her relationship with Indra and Vishnu, is as much about economics as it is about women. Is wealth (women) simply a commodity, to be consumed and controlled? Or is wealth (women) a reflection of who we are: the more we understand wealth (women), the more we understand ourselves?

Here is a story from the Lakshmi Purana, which was composed about 400 years ago, in Odisha.

Balarama, the elder brother of Jagannath, who is Vishnu, once saw Lakshmi enter the house of a *chandala*. In the Hindu caste spectrum, chandalas are opposite of Brahmins, associated with work involving garbage, sewage and dead bodies of humans and animals. Balarama said Lakshmi had become impure and should not be allowed to enter the temple. Jagannath obeyed his elder brother and shut the door on Lakshmi's face. From that day onwards, the two brothers had no access to food. There was nothing in the kitchen, in the pantry, in the markets, or in the fields or orchards. Balarama realized that notions of purity and impurity, that provide fodder to the ego, make no sense to the body. Balarama had no choice but to open the door and let Lakshmi in.

A bowl of rice will not distinguish between the rich and the poor, the pure and the impure, the powerful and the powerless. Rice in a golden bowl tastes no different from the one served on a leaf. That is why, even today, food eaten by devotees in the temple of Jagannath is often offered on broken pottery. Thus, the Lakshmi Purana uses the Goddess to present the idea of equality. She treats everyone equally. Lakshmi lore also presents the idea of freedom. Humans can create boundaries and rules, and transform food into property, something over which we have rights.

Devdutt Pattanaik

But Lakshmi does not differentiate between the owner and the thief. She will satisfy the hunger of whosoever consumes her. Morality, ethics, justice, and concepts like caste, creed, religion, come from the world of gods, from the world of Indra and Vishnu, Brahma and Shiva.

And yet, Lakshmi loves Vishnu more than others. Why? For he understands her need to be free. And he understands the value she brings to the table. She takes away hunger. She provides comfort. But humans turn food into something else—a tool to indulge the ego and feel superior to other humans, by clinging to her, hoarding her, not sharing her with others.

In nature, food flows from the weak to the strong, from the old to the young, from the stupid to the smart. This gives rise to the food chain, which is full of predators and prey. This gives rise to the pecking order, where the strong dominates and establishes territory, and corners all the food and mates. This is the natural world of fish justice (*matsya nyaya*). Humans are not supposed to live like this. Humans have the wherewithal to outgrow these animal instincts: instead of focusing on our own hunger, we can focus on other people's hunger. Dharma happens when the world where 'eaters are eaten' becomes the world where 'feeders are fed'. When humans refuse to elevate themselves so, it is adharma.

This idea is the cornerstone of Vedic thought. It is ritually expressed in the Vedic ritual of yagna, where the yajaman (householder) feeds the devata (deity) and the pitr (ancestor), and hopes to be fed in return. This ritual is established by Brahma himself. Daksha feeds Indra and Indra feeds him in return. Unfortunately, we find both these gods losing their primary position over time. In Buddhist and Jain lore, both are shown bowing to monks. In the Hindu Purana, both are inferior to Shiva and Vishnu. Shiva beheads Brahma, and his son, Prajapati Daksha. Vishnu is kinder, for he recognizes the insecurity that prompts Brahma and Indra to behave as they do.

Neither Brahma nor Indra value the Goddess.

- Brahma chases Saraswati, who refuses to be domesticated.

- Brahma's son, Daksha, tries to control Sati, who wants to choose her own groom.

- Brahma's grandson, Kashyapa's son, Indra, fails to understand Sachi and wonders why she always wants to slip away.

In nature, food is not shared. Humans can share food. From Brahma (via Daksha, Kashyapa and other Prajapatis) come the diverse organisms (jiva) of the world. Every organism seeks food. Since we all come from the same original source, we can say plants, animals and humans are a family, with a common ancestry. Hence the Sanskrit phrase 'vasudhaiva kutumbakam', the world is my family.

All living beings inherit the earth. No one has greater right to it than the other. In the plant and the animal world, all organisms that eat food end up being eaten as food. But in the human world, we protect ourselves from being eaten, by exchanging goods and services. As long as I feed you and you feed me, there is collaboration, and all is well. But the moment one child hoards all the food and does not feed the other child, in order to dominate, he creates a hierarchy, which eventually leads to violence. When traders turn into tricksters, then one party hoards and the other starves. This causes trading to be replaced by raiding. There is war over Lakshmi, over land, over cattle and over women.

In Vedic literature, Indra is the great warrior god who overpowers asuras and claims all the cows. In Brahmana literature, Indra uses trickery, to corner all the food, leaving nothing for asuras. In Puranic literature, as well as Buddhist and Jain lore, we find description of Indra's paradise, where all resources are cornered. These are:

- The wish-fulfilling tree, Kalpataru.
- The wish-fulfilling cow, Kamadhenu.
- The wish-fulfilling jewel, Chintamani.
- The cornucopia overflowing with gold and grain, Akshay Patra.

This is contrasted by three kinds of hell also found in Puranic literature, as well as Buddhist and Jain lore:

- *Patala*, the realm of asuras, located under the ground, where the sun does not shine. In that realm, Lakshmi is Pulomi, daughter of the asura. Her true value emerges only when she is extracted out from under the earth in the form of water, minerals, gems and the harvest of seeds sown. The devas, who live in the sky, extract this value and take Lakshmi to their celestial realm where she becomes Sachi, Indra's wife. Patala then becomes a metaphor for the realm of those exploited for resources.

- *Naraka* is the realm of those trapped in debt. This is a mercantile concept. What is credit and debit in the material world becomes *punya* and *paap* in the spiritual world of the karmic balance sheet. Those who give credit rise to swarga and those who have debts sink into naraka. This is best explained by the snake and ladder game where snake is debit/paap and the ladder is credit/punya. This becomes a metaphor for the realm of those reduced to bonded labour by moneylenders.

- Pirt-loka is the realm of the dead, those who await rebirth. This becomes a metaphor for the realm of the future generation, that awaits impatiently to take over their reins of the world. But the old refuse to let go; they cling to wealth and power, like the banyan tree that will not let anything grow in its shadow.

Indra's swarga or paradise is not the highest realm. It's a temporary refuge for those who have a lot of credit in their karmic balance sheet. The higher heaven is the one where there is no debit or credit, where there is loan to repay to creditors or loan to reclaim from debtors. in Jainism, this realm is described as Siddha-loka, in Buddhism as Buddha-loka and in Hinduism as Kailasa-loka of Shiva. This is the realm of contentment. Indra was not content despite having everything. He was terrified that the unfaithful Lakshmi would run away from his realm. Instead of making himself worthy of her affection, he spent all his time defeating rivals who also wished to grab and hoard her. His throne wobbled in three situations:

- When a rival king performed more yagna than he did and became preferred by Brahmins over him. This is the realm of competition in the marketplace, where dominant players seek monopoly.

- When an asura rose from patala and demanded his share of the Lakshmi extracted. He asked Brahma, Vishnu, Shiva and Devi to kill this asura. But they kept coming back. These asuras insisted that Lakshmi belonged to them; she was their daughter, their sister. They had as much right over her as Indra, her husband. This was the realm of family disputes over property.

- When a hermit stopped performing yagna and practised tapasya. When, instead of seeking the wealth and pleasures from swarga, he sought to outgrow hunger and desire itself. He sent damsels to enchant such a person, to remind him how delightful Lakshmi was. This is the realm where advertising was used to stoke flagging demand.

Indra became a metaphor for humans who focused only on their hunger, so much so that they forgot contentment and the needs of others. Such men do not see women as humans, as hungry and insecure as they are, but simply as service providers, playing the role of mothers, daughters, wives, lovers and sisters. For Indra, Lakshmi was nothing but food for his consumption, to be hoarded to enable his domination. Vishnu saw Lakshmi as both, an object to be consumed and a subject that sought to consume. He recognized that he too was Lakshmi. While, like Shiva, the Buddha and the Jina, he could be a consumer, who found contentment, he could also be the commodity that others wanted to consume.

In temple lore, there is a footprint on the shoulder of Vishnu. It is the mark of Bhrigu, who kicked Vishnu awake.

Bhrigu was irritated that none of the three gods of the Hindu trinity were paying him attention. Vishnu apologized. Bhrigu then pointed to the fate of Lakshmi. With no one paying attention to her, she was going around the world spreading havoc. Those who had her were consumed by pride and arrogance. Those who did not have her were consumed by anger and jealousy. This was spreading conflict and competition everywhere. The world was an unhappy place. He wanted Vishnu to go down to earth and make Lakshmi happy.

How does one make Lakshmi happy? Lakshmi is happiest when she is given away. The giver earns credit and rises to heaven; the receiver gets into debt and descends towards hell. To prevent the descent, the receiver repays his debt. That way, Lakshmi moves again and the unburdened receiver rises again, towards heaven.

Unfortunately, the world is full of people eager to grab Lakshmi, hold Lakshmi, bind Lakshmi, rather than letting her go to others and bringing joy into their lives.

- The devas claim and consume Lakshmi.
- The asuras fight to get back Lakshmi.
- The rakshasas steal Lakshmi.
- The yakshas hoard Lakshmi.

And those who give, do not demand her return. Laskhmi needs to fall like rain and flow like a river. But she also needs to rise back up like moisture, pulled up by the sun, transforming into clouds. Only Vishnu enables this. For this Vishnu took the form of fish.

Vishnu was a fish who asked Manu to save him from the big fish. Manu did that, transferring him from the dangers of the open waters to the safety of a pot. When the fish became big enough to fend for himself, Manu let him return to the waters. When a flood threatened to drown Manu, the big fish saved him. Thus, Vishnu encouraged people to help the helpless; he also repaid his debts. This is dharma, the exchange that is the cornerstone of culture.

He also took the form of a turtle.

Vishnu was the turtle who helped the devas and the asuras churn out Lakshmi from the ocean of milk. He enabled it but did not seek the output— Lakshmi. The devas claimed her but did not share her. The asuras fought to get her. Vishnu did not seek Lakshmi because he was content: he knew who he was and who Lakshmi was. He knew Lakshmi existed only to take away the hunger of the body. She could not take away insecurities. She could not give humans meaning. Vishnu knew he was not a function of what he had or did not have. So, he did not seek to grab, hold and hoard Lakshmi, denying others. The deva and the asura, on the other hand, believed they were defined by what they had and what they do not have. They saw what Lakshmi could do for them. Vishnu saw what he could do for Lakshmi. He could give Lakshmi meaning by giving her to someone who sought to consume her and not possess her to give himself meaning.

He then took the form of a wild boar.

Vishnu rescued the earth in the form of a boar and promised to protect her from those who wanted to plunder her. She was the cow and he, her cowherd.

He protected her and she nourished him. Thus, there was the perfect symbiotic exchange. He descended in mortal form, as Ram and Krishna, to save the earth from kings who abused her. Ram and Krishna are therefore never shown as ambitious: seeking Lakshmi. They were content. They simply ensured others gave Lakshmi the respect she was due.

Vishnu was the wily one, who tricked the trickster. Brahma, the hungry and insecure one, only took. Shiva, the guileless one, only gave. Vishnu demanded that what was taken, or given, was eventually returned. That was the only way to ensure Lakshmi was always moving and never hoarded. If you only give, you will never be the child who receives. If you only take, you will never be the parent who gives.

In Vishnu temples, Lakshmi is always enshrined outside Vishnu's shrine. For he always gives her away and ensures her movement. When you give Lakshmi away, you earn credit and rise up towards Vaikuntha. Those who receive Lakshmi end up in debt and descend down, either towards naraka, full of suffering, or swarga, full of strife. Suffering continues till debts are repaid. It ends when there is contentment and Lakshmi is shared. Those who invest in others, help them repay their debts, discover contentment and the joy of investing in others, are Lakshmi's beloved. For they liberate the restless one, so she can be her true self.

When telling stories about Lakshmi, are storytellers referring to wealth, women or women-as-wealth or wealth-as-goddess? One cannot help but wonder. The stories are gendered, but the ideas are gender-neutral. But it is easy to confuse and conflate. So, we need to pause and be alert to the differentiation.

7

Woman as Metaphor

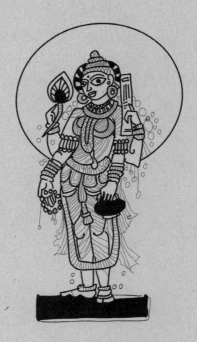

Knowledge was first embodied as a goddess by Jains, visualized as holding a book and memory beads.

Images of Saraswati, the goddess of knowledge, are often placed in libraries, right next to the board that says 'Silence Please'. No one notices that the Goddess always holds a musical instrument called veena (lute) in her hand. The irony is lost on many who look at sacred images without actually doing darshan.

Darshan is the act of seeing that generates insight and results in reflection. For example, the sight of the veena grants us some insight into the human ability to make music and musical instruments, and this makes us reflect on how music made by humans is different from the music made by birds. The music of birds is specific, to enable survival. It is designed to attract mates and draw attention of fellow birds to food or predators. Human music, on the other hand, is not necessary for survival. But it adds beauty to life and makes us wonder about the meaning of existence, by making us aware of various rhythms and emotions.

Unlike other goddesses, there are not many stories about Saraswati. She is more the embodiment of a concept.

Saraswati is draped in a white sari indicating she has distanced herself from the materialistic world, represented by colourful fabrics. While Lakshmi nourishes the body with food, Saraswati nourishes the mind with knowledge and the arts. Lakshmi's wealth is contained in a pot; Saraswati's knowledge is expressed through words, through songs, stories and music, dance and arts. In Jain art, the more austere Digambar monks compared Saraswati to a peacock while the white-clad Shwetambar monks compared her to a goose (*hamsa*). In Indian folklore, dancing peacocks attract rain clouds, while hamsas are able to separate milk from water, like fact from fiction.

- The peacock links Saraswati to art, dance, music, theatre and entertainment.
- The hamsa links Saraswati to ideas embodied within, and communicated through sounds, songs, stories, songs, symbols and gestures: the knowledge of maths, science, literature and philosophy.

Saraswati is therefore linked to both, the peacock-like courtesans as well as the swan-like philosophers. In modern society, the courtesan has been erased from history, her contributions to the world of art appropriated by men.

In popular Hindu mythology, Saraswati is called the wife of Brahma. But she is also called the daughter of Brahma. This can be confusing. The confusion comes from our failure to appreciate that mythology is metaphorical. Gods and goddesses are given supernatural forms so that we appreciate the idea, the symbol and do not take things literally. That Saraswati is shown with four hands, and Brahma with four heads, is the clue provided by the artist that these figures embody ideas, not entities.

Human ideas are complex. Words are often not enough to communicate an idea. We need grammar. We need sentences. We need punctuation. We shift from prose to poetry, we use music and melody, even gestures and symbols, to communicate subtle, refined ideas. Language has metaphors where known words are used to explain and elaborate unknown ideas and inexpressible emotions. Still ideas resist transmission. What is conveyed by the source is not received by the destination.

To communicate Vedic ideas to people, the sages decided to compose stories. Ideas then become characters. The relationship between ideas is communicated through relationships among characters. Characters have gender, and so the relationship between ideas ends up being expressed in sexual terms. When the characters are gods, indicated by their supernatural form, they serve as metaphors. They are vehicles for ideas that resist simple communication.

Veda, which means knowledge, pays a lot of attention to the reality that is visible and the reality that is not visible.

- Food is a reality that is visible. It is visualized in female form as Lakshmi, the goddess of fortune. The name Lakshmi is derived from 'laksha', which means target.

- Hunger is a reality that is invisible. It is visualized in male form as Indra, the master of paradise, where all fortune is cornered. The name Indra is derived from 'indriya', which means sense.

- Indra chasing Lakshmi is then a metaphor for hunger chasing food.

- Indra rides elephants. The aroused, excited, uncontrollable elephant in the state of *masht* is how the poets describe Madan, or Kama, the god of uncontrollable craving.

- Shiva, who burns Madan, then embodies the mind that controls craving.

- Shiva also beheads Brahma's fifth head that sprouts as he chases Saraswati. Here, Brahma views Saraswati as entertainment to be consumed, rather than knowledge that will help him evolve.

- In wisdom, Brahma realizes that the point of creation is to feed the other. Animals eat and are eaten, but humans need to feed and be fed. This applies to food, as well as to power and knowledge. Saraswati created must be given away. In the process we gain insight and reflection.

Male forms are consistently used to depict mental states:

1. Brahma for craving

2. Indra for insecurity

3. Vishnu for empathy

4. Shiva for indifference

5. Kartikeya for restraint

6. Ganesha for contentment

Female forms are consistently used to depict material states.

1. Kali for the wild

2. Gauri for the cultivated

3. Lakshmi for resources

4. Saraswati for communication

5. Durga for battle

6. Uma for household

7. Annapurna for kitchen

8. Chamundi for crematorium

Why are male forms used to depict the invisible reality of the mind and female forms for the visible reality of matter? The reason is relatively simple if one appreciates the male and female anatomy from the point of view of the artist and the storyteller, who carry the burden of communicating Vedic ideas.

- The male body lends itself to symbolize invisible states of the mind (hunger). The male body transforms dramatically when aroused. The erect penis denotes attraction. The flaccid penis denotes lack of interest. The spurting of semen is used by artists and storytellers as a tool to explain temptation. The hermit with shut eyes but erect penis indicates someone indifferent to everyone in the external world, but at bliss in his own internal world. We are the Brahma who chases his own daughter, Shiva who rejects his own wife and Vishnu who dances with his sister.

- The female body lends itself to symbolize the visible states of matter (food). The female body transforms dramatically when it becomes pregnant or when it does not get pregnant. When life is created within the female body, the belly expands for all to see. When life is not created within the body, menstrual blood flows for all to see. The female form becomes the world we are born into. As Mangala–Gauri she nurtures us and as Chamunda–Kali she consumes us. We experience her as the wild Vana-chandi (forest), the violent Rana-chandi (conflict zone), and the secure and nourishing Mangala-chandi (garden).

That is how Saraswati clarifies pronouns. She gives male pronouns to thoughts and female pronouns to things in the Puranic world. From thoughts come things and from things come thoughts. Hunger makes us seek food, food ends up amplifying hunger and inspiring the mind to come up with innovative ideas related to the generation and distribution of food. In other words, when the male and female pronouns come together, life happens. That is what we discover from Saraswati.

A cigar is sometimes just a cigar. But a woman is sometimes not just a woman. She is an idea. And when she is an idea, she needs to be appreciated within the cultural context.

- Eve communicates a Middle Eastern idea, not a global one.

- Pandora communicates a Greek idea, not a global one.

- Isis communicates an Egyptian idea, not a global one.

- Saraswati communicates an Indian idea, not a global one.

The idea of monomyth—the hero's journey—established by Joseph Campbell and popularized by Hollywood, since the 1970s, is not only patriarchal but also culturally insensitive. The idea of the hero is alien to Hindu thought, simply because Hindu mythology is rooted in the idea of rebirth, which is alien to the West.

Rebirth takes away the burden of a starting point (Creation, Big Bang) or end point (Apocalypse). God therefore is very different in Hinduism as compared to God in monotheistic faiths. In Catholic art, God is an old White man. God in Hinduism cannot be explained without considering the Goddess. And Goddess, spelt with a capital G, is very different from goddess.

- Middle Eastern mythology (Judaism, Christian and Islam) has neither Goddess nor goddesses.

- Greek mythology has many goddesses (Olympians, Titans) but no Goddess.

- Egyptian mythology has no concept of God or Goddess, only gods and goddesses, some more powerful than others.

The God of Hinduism is not the all-powerful being of Jewish, Christian or Islamic faiths, who created the world. In Hinduism, the Goddess is called the primal one, Adya, who always exists. Attempts to make Brahma the 'creator' of Hindu mythology is simply colonial hangover, the assumption of universality. Men like Freud and Jung, who focused on Biblical and Christian mythology, belonged to imperial times, when European ideas were deemed universal and European archetypes became universal architypes. The use of European framework does not let one do 'darshan' of Hindu mythology.

In Hindu stories, Brahma is beheaded and not worshipped as he declares himself 'creator' of the Goddess and at the same time seeks to consume her, thus indulging in 'incest'. The creator cannot be the consumer, says Hindu philosophy. In nature, we exist for others. What we create must be consumed by others. We have to feed others and others have to feed us. Flowers and fruits of a tree are consumed by insects, birds and other animals. While hermit orders focus on the self, the householder orders of India focus on the other. The hermit seeks to outgrow his own hunger; the householder is expected to outgrow his own hunger while satisfying the hunger of others. Brahma's creation must be consumed by the other. If Brahma consumes what he creates, he does not use the full potential of the human mind.

The idea of a goddess resisting control and seeking freedom is a recurring theme in Hindu mythology. We can see this literally — women resisting patriarchy. Or we can see this metaphorically — wealth, power and knowledge, embodied in Lakshmi, Durga and Saraswati, need to be distributed not hoarded. They must be allowed to flow like a river if they have to nourish life. Here is a story from the mountains of Jammu.

Vedavati was meditating, seeking Vishnu as a husband, when Bhairava spotted her and asked her to be his partner in Tantrik rites. She refused. He tried to catch her by force. She ran. He pursued. After many adventures, she finally turned around, picked up a sword and severed his head from his body. She became a goddess on top of the mountain while Bhairava's severed head, found below the mountain, worshipped her, like the fifth head of Brahma, who realized she is the goddess who grants wisdom when observed, not consumed.

Devdutt Pattanaik

A similar story is told in the mountains of Garhwal.

A demon took the form of a bull and chased the two sisters Nanda and Sunanda, determined to possess them. The sisters ran away. They sought help from plants—the yam, the turmeric, the wheat, the pine tree. But none protected them. None hid them. So the sisters cursed them that they would be cut, pounded and threshed by humans. The banana plant hid them behind the leaves but a goat ate the leaves and exposed the girls. The girls blessed the banana plant that she would be considered sacred by all. They cursed the goat that she would be slaughtered in village ceremonies. Finally, the sisters picked up a trident and impaled the bull-demon. They would not be forced into submission. They would domesticate themselves voluntarily, out of love and affection.

Both stories resonate a theme found in the oldest Vedic texts.

When Brahma awoke, he realized he was alone. Lonely, he created beings from his mind—the mind-born sages. But they did not take away his misery. Then he saw a woman walking around him. He tried to catch her. She ran away. He pursued her. She kept taking forms of various female beasts and he became the corresponding male. She was the cow;

he became the bull. She was the mare; he became the horse. She was the goose; he became the gander. The mind-born sages were horrified. Then Rudra appeared and pinned Brahma to the skies with his arrow. Brahma sprouted four more heads to gaze upon the goddess. Bhairava appeared and severed the fifth head. Thus was Brahma tempered, but declared unworthy of worship.

When the Purana states that Brahma creates the world, Vishnu sustains the world and Shiva destroys the world, it is important to keep in mind what is being created here. Not nature, but culture. The 'men' here represent the human mind.

- Brahma first uses force and is beheaded. He then establishes the ritual of exchange (yagna) to distinguish humans from animals. Animals grab food. Humans can give and receive food. But he does it as a patriarch, to feed himself. He is the consumer, the *bhogi*.

- Shiva destroys this culture of consumption (*bhoga*) as the hermit who shuns food and seeks to destroy hunger through the practice of tapasya (churning of inner fire). Shiva is thus tapasvi.

- Vishnu balances the two by becoming the householder who promotes contentment over craving. He is the yogi, who empathizes with the bhogis around him.

He connects the otherwise disconnected self and the desolate other. In the animal world, the other is only opportunity (food, ally, mate) or threat (predator, rival). Vishnu recognizes that the other is like the self — hungry and frightened, seeking meaning.

We can say that Shiva embodies indifference and Vishnu embodies empathy. Both these concepts are difficult to express in art. So Shiva is shown relaxed atop a mountain of snow, a cold place without plants or water. Shiva seeks neither food nor clothing or shelter. He is Maha-dev, who wants nothing. But he is also indifferent to those around him. The Goddess draws his attention to the other. Hence 'marriage', which is a metaphor for the self to connect with the other. She is the other. The ghosts (*pret*) who surround him are the other. His children are the other. He may be content, but he needs to have empathy for their craving.

When Vishnu sleeps, the mind sleeps, empathy sleeps, and the self becomes self-indulgent. The self assumes the world exists for his own consumption. This delusion of the world is called Maya (delusion). Here Brahma chases the Goddess and gets hurt.

When Vishnu awakens, empathy is restored, and the world no longer enchants, it enlightens. This world that teaches us is Vidya (knowledge). The Goddess is thus both delusion and knowledge, based on whether Vishnu sleeps (we are consumed by our own hunger) or Vishnu is awake (we are sensitive to, and concerned about, other people's hunger).

We want the sleeping God to wake up. That is why Kali danced atop Shiva's chest, turned the corpse (shava) into the awakened divine (*shiva*), so that he placed her on his lap to become Uma-Shankar. Sleeping Vishnu, i.e. Narayana, is visualized with four arms reclining on the coils of a multi-headed serpent, fantastic imagery again, a code reminding us that what is being shown is not to be taken literally but to be unravelled metaphorically. We must never let our pronouns limit us.

8

Object of Her Desire

*Acknowledgement of female desire and woman's pleasure
is a key theme on temple walls.*

This is a story where a woman's desire triumphed.

Usha was the daughter of an asura king called Bana, who lived in Pragjyotisha, a city on the eastern side of India. She asked for paintings of the most handsome men on earth and fell in love with Anirudh, the grandson of Krishna, who lived in Dwarka, on the western side of India. She got him abducted and brought to her palace. Her father did not approve of the match and had Anirudh thrown in jail. Anirudh's father, Pradyumna, and grandfather, Krishna, flew into the city on the eagle Garuda. They defeated Bana and united the lovers. Usha was happy.

Usha's pleasure (*vilasa*) was a popular theme in ancient Indian art. This acknowledgement of a woman's desire was not an act of subversion or rebellion, it was the most natural thing. The satisfaction of women's desire was deemed good (*shubh*) and auspicious (*mangala*). It brought happiness (*kalyan*) and satisfaction (*samadhan*) to all.

In the Ramayana, Ravana is shown surrounded by many women. In the Bhagavata, Krishna is shown surrounded by many women too. But the two contexts are very different. The women of Lanka exist for the satisfaction of Ravana, but Krishna exists for the delight of the women in Madhuvana and Dwarka.

Hence, he multiplies himself to ensure each one of them feels fulfilled.

In the twentieth century, archaeologists in India found terracotta images of women with legs spread apart, their heads and vulvas replaced by lotus flowers. There was no text associated with this image. They are mostly dated to around the eighth century, a time which saw a proliferation of goddess images in Hindu, Buddhist and Jain art. The following story was associated with this image.

> One day, Shiva and Shakti were making love when the Seven Sages paid them a visit. Shiva did not stop. Shakti, embarrassed, covered her face with a lotus flower.

The archaeologists decided to name the image Lajjagauri. Lajja means shame or modesty. Gauri means a mother. The image was declared a fertility symbol. No one considered the possibility that it simply revealed the desire of a woman for pleasure, not pregnancy.

In Indian mythology, women are not asexual beings or simply prey for sexual predators. They do not exist just to produce babies. They have desires that can be acknowledged, feared, indulged, restrained, violated or suppressed. In the Mahabharata, we find questions like: Who enjoys sex more, man or woman? In response, Bhishma tells the story of Bangashwana.

There was a man who was cursed by Indra to become a woman. As a man, he had sex with women, as a woman, he had sex with men. He was asked if he got greater pleasure when he had a male body or when he had a female body. Bangashwana said he had greater pleasure when he had a female body.

The story declares that women have greater sexual appetite than men. However, the story is sometimes told in a different way.

As a man, Bangashwana had children who called him Father, as a woman, he had children who called him Mother. When asked which body was superior, male or female, Bangashwana said, 'The female body, because the sound of a mother is sweeter than the sound of a father.'

Unlike the first version, where a woman's desire is acknowledged, the second version limits a woman's joy to motherhood. That two versions exist indicates a tension in Indian society between patriarchy that seeks to control the body of a woman, tame it, use it, like a farmer uses a field, and feminism that seeks to grant woman agency over her own body, allows her to bloom and enjoy the pleasure of bees and butterflies.

That a woman's desire for sex is greater than a man's was a common belief in ancient society. Here is a story from the Jaiminiya Brahmana, composed before 500 BC (2,500 years ago).

> From Indra's thigh was born the handsome Kutsa so handsome that he looked just like Indra. When Indra found Sachi with Kutsa he was furious. 'But he looks just like you,' she said. So Indra made Kutsa bald, but he still found Sachi with Kutsa. 'But he covered his head with a turban and he looks just like you.' So Indra put dirt between Kutsa's shoulder blades, but he still found Sachi with Kutsa. 'But he wore an upper garment and he looks just like you.'

In this story, Indra is irritated with his rival, not his wife. Later, Kutsa is sent on an errand. His beauty is weaponized.

The handsome Kutsa was sent by Indra to seduce and pin down the offering-stealing demoness whose appetite for food was matched by her appetite for sex. The demoness was called Dirgha-jivhi, which means someone with a long tongue. She told Kutsa that he had only one sexual organ but she had many so he wouldn't be able to satisfy her. So Indra gave Kutsa a sexual organ on every limb for the pleasure of Dirgha-jivhi. She accepted him and he pinned her to the ground, enabling Indra to throw his weapon and kill her.

The Mahabharata, composed at least five centuries after these Brahmana texts, narrates stories acknowledging the sexual tension between a guru's young student and the guru's young wife.

- Rishi Devasharma's wife, Ruchi, was drawn to Indra in his absence. To prevent her from committing an act of adultery, Devasharma's student Vipula used his yogic powers to enter her mind. He restrained her from succumbing to temptation.

- Rishi Veda's wife tried to seduce her student Uttanaka when her husband was away. When he shunned her advances, she punished him by asking him to give as his tuition fee (guru-dakshina) the earrings of the wife of the fearsome cannibal king Saudasa.

In the Ramayana, when Gautama found his wife in the arms of Indra, he refused to believe that she was tricked and cursed her to turn her into stone. This story foreshadows the doubt of the people of Ayodhya when Ram returned with Sita by his side. The people wondered if Sita, locked in Ravana's pleasure garden for four months, could have stayed true to her husband, evidence notwithstanding. In both these stories, the underlying assumption is that women have a great sexual appetite that demands satisfaction.

Tales of sexually frustrated, unfaithful wives abound in Indian folklore. *Sukasaptati* (Seventy Tales of the Parrot) is a collection of seventy Sanskrit stories narrated by a parrot. Parrot is the favourite bird of the love god Kama, i.e. Ananga. The frame story of this collection involves a merchant.

A merchant was going away on travel. He felt that while he was away, travelling across the sea for trade, his wife would be lonely at home. He was also anxious that she would be unable to control her desires and would form relationships with other men. So, he left his parrot behind, to remind her of her promise to be faithful to him. To stop the woman from going to the house of her lover at night, the parrot told her erotic tales. These were stories of frustrated wives, angry husbands, adultery, heartbreak and the dangers of not respecting the laws of marriage. The stories were full of humour, mischief and trickery. There was no moral judgement.

While a faithful wife is desired, venerated and even worshipped, the unfaithful woman is not seen as evil. She is just seen as someone who is unable to control her natural desires. Sexual longings of unmarried and married women gave rise to the *akam* (interior) poems of Tamil Sangam literature, which are about 1800 years old. Similar sentiments manifest in Prakrit poetry, *Gaha Saptasati*.

We have all heard of the *Kama-sutra* (a string of rules for pleasure), a book written for the satisfaction of men. But there was another book called *Ananga-ranga* (love god's sport), written for the satisfaction of women.

Once upon a time, a woman walked naked into the king's court. The king was alarmed at her behaviour. The woman said, 'I'm a married woman, I have been told I have to be faithful to my husband. But my husband does not satisfy me sexually. Is there anyone in this land who can satisfy me sexually? If a husband does not satisfy his wife sexually, how can he expect his wife to be faithful to him?' The king realized that it was a valid point. He asked his ministers to create an erotic manual that men could read to satisfy their wives, to keep their wives faithful.

In this story, the burden of fidelity is not with the woman but with the man. Only a man who satisfies his wife can expect her to be faithful to him in return. Saubhari, an old sage, who married fifty daughters of a king, made himself virile and multiplied himself fifty times so that all the women were fully satisfied. The moon god was cursed to wane because he was unable to satisfy all his wives. The moon sought the help of Shiva to replenish himself so that he could satisfy them all.

- Shiva's unhappy wife is presented as Kali, angry, with hair unbound and tongue sticking out.
- Shiva's satisfied wife is presented as Gauri, content, with her hair tied and a smile on her face.

As patriarchy rose, as feudalism was established in India, for economic and political reasons, elite women were not allowed to choose their own husbands. She was given away by her father to a groom of his choice or sold to the highest bidder or given away as trophy in a martial competition, or taken away from her father by force. But there is memory of a time when a woman was not chattel. Her desire mattered.

In the oldest narration of the Ramayana, which is 2000 years old, we are told that Sita was a trophy in an archery competition. Whosoever strung Shiva's bow would marry her. Yet in Sanskrit plays, which are 1500 years old, we find variations to this tale. Sita meets Ram in a garden before the competition, falls in love with him, wants to be with him and hopes he will win the competition. Here we see the earliest documented tension between arranged marriages and love marriages.

The failure to satisfy the sexual desire of women generates rage and violence. In south India, we find stories where sexual satisfaction ends the aggression of a queen.

Queen Meenakshi of Madurai was a violent three-breasted princess who went around defeating kings in battle. Her conquests brought her to the north. She saw Shiva atop the Himalayas. Spellbound by his beauty, she lost her extra breast and her desire for violence. She asked Shiva to come to the city of Madurai and live as her consort. He agreed. He resides as Somasundara in a small temple next to hers. Every night he comes to her, but only after she has completed her royal duties. The priests of the Goddess temple welcome her husband. His presence ensures she is benevolent and measured, and not wild.

In another story, marriage is prevented so that the Goddess can stay violent and defend the gods.

Kanyakumari stood on the southern tip of India, waiting for Shiva to marry her. The gods did not want her to marry. Marriage would distract her and dilute her extraordinary martial powers, that the gods needed in their battle against demons. So they tricked Shiva into turning back. A frustrated Kanyakumari threw away all the food that had been cooked for the wedding and wiped away her make-up. This is why, we are told, that the sea and the sand on the southern tip of India is so colourful.

The sexually demanding woman was gradually seen as threat to monks, especially since restraint and discipline made monks more attractive. So Buddhist tales speak of women as sexual predators who demanded satisfaction at all cost.

- In Sulasa Jataka, a courtesan rescued a criminal using her wealth and influence as she desired him. Later, she killed him, when he tried to kill her and take her wealth.

- Kanavera Jataka tells a similar tale: Here, a thief, rescued by a courtesan, ran away from her fearing she who had killed her earlier lover to save him, could in the future kill him to secure another lover.

- In Harita Jataka, an ascetic found the queen bathing in the royal orchard. They ended up having sex. When the king returned from battle and learnt of the affair, he forgave them both.

- In Mudulakkhana Jataka, the demands of the queen made the infatuated ascetic regain his senses, give up on his desire for her and return to the ascetic path.

- In Mahapaduma Jataka, the queen falsely accused her stepson, the prince, of raping her because he rejected her sexual proposition.

- In Bandhanamokka Jataka, in a similar story, the queen wanted her husband to be faithful but, while he was away in battle, had sex with all his messengers and even tried to seduce his minister who resisted her advances.

- Kosiya Jataka tells the story of a wicked wife who pretended to be sick all day to sleep so that at night she could stay awake while her husband was sleeping and meet her lovers.

- In Culla-Kunala Jataka, a wife left her husband to have sex with her lovers, washed herself and returned to bed. But her cold body under the blanket made the husband suspicious.

- Takka Jataka tells the story of a woman who had sex with a man who saved her from drowning, and later with the thief who abducted her.

- Andabhuta Jataka tells the story of how a gambler won the game of dice with a mantra that derived its power from the infidelity of women.

- Age has no impact on the libido of women. So the Susima Jataka narrates the tale of an old queen mother who wanted to marry her son's young friend who was also the royal priest. To force the young man to marry his mother, the king gave up his crown.

- Asatamanta Jataka tells the story of the old mother of a teacher who fell in love with a student assigned to take care of her.

- Perhaps the most vivid tale of female infidelity is in the Kunala Jataka, where the Bodhisattva himself, in the form of a cuckoo, told eight stories of unfaithful, lustful, untrustworthy women.

In Jain stories, when husbands and sons become monks, women respond differently. Some accept this and even become nuns. In one story, a nun starved herself to death to stop her husband from breaking his monastic vows. In another, wives are not so supportive.

A monk's wife turned into a tigress and attacked her own son who had joined the monastery like his father, leaving her alone. Another turned into a goddess and tormented her former husband, by making his body get aroused in public despite his total lack of arousal. This was embarrassing for the monk, but he maintained his calm and cool and didn't berate the goddess who was his ex-wife. He understood her frustration and forgave her.

Positively or negatively, these stories acknowledge the desire of a woman. Jain mythology refers to Kamadeva, men who are as beautiful as the god of love. Wherever these men go, women wish to marry them.

Krishna's father, Vasudeva, was a Kamadeva. In his past life he was so ugly that no woman desired him. He spent his time serving a Jain monk who offered him a divine form in his next life. But he wished to be reborn as a stunningly handsome man who could break the heart of every woman he met. So he was born as a handsome prince. His elder brother told him not to leave the palace as the sun would damage his beauty. Later, he learnt that his brother had said this to prevent him from roaming the streets of the city and distracting the women of the land with his irresistible beauty. Feeling embarrassed, Vasudeva left his brother's kingdom and travelled the world. Wherever he went women chased him.

Vasudeva's adventures with women gave rise to an entire collection of stories known as *Vasudeva-hindi* (Wanderings of Vasudeva). Vasudeva's son, Balarama, was also a very handsome man. But he did not wish to be the object of women's desire.

Once, Balarama was meditating in a village when he noticed that the village women would keep staring at him, spellbound by his beauty. One woman was collecting water from a well, but instead of putting the rope around the pot, she put the rope around her child's neck. So distracting was Balarama's beauty. Realizing the harm his beauty could cause, Balarama decided to meditate facing the mountain so nobody could see his face.

In the Ramayana, many women wanted to marry Ram. But Ram would always clarify that he was married to Sita and was determined to be faithful to her.

- When Vedavati approached Ram he told her that he would forever be faithful to Sita. She would have to wait until he returned on earth as Krishna.

- Surpanakha, who did not care for consent, forced herself on Ram and Lakshman. The resulting violence, the chopping of her nose, set in motion a series of events that brought unhappiness to all.

In the Mahabharata, we learn how Arjuna was approached by many women.

- Uloopi forced him to give her a child.

- Subhadra eloped with him.

- Chitrangada was willing to shed her masculine nature and be more feminine for him.

- The apsara Urvashi wanted to be intimate with Arjuna, but when he refused on the grounds that she, an immortal being, had once been the lover of his ancestor, Pururava. An angry Urvashi cursed him to become a eunuch.

When he was leaving for exile, Nakul smeared his face with dust to stop women from following him. Such was his beauty that women would follow him everywhere. A folklore called Jambul Akhyan, from

Maharashtra, informs us how Draupadi was not content despite having five husbands.

Draupadi once accidentally plucked a fruit that a sage wanted to eat. He threatened her with a curse if she did not refix the fruit to the tree. The only way to do that was by being honest and revealing her deepest secret. She admitted, therefore, that she still desired Karna, the charioteer's son, who could not marry her because of his low social status. The five Pandavas were upset by her admission, but then Krishna told them to eat the fruit now refixed to the tree. If their tongue turned purple (the fruit was the Indian blackberry or jambul), it meant they all had transgressive longings in their heart.

Jambul always stains the tongue purple. A reminder that we all have sexual desires that do not align with cultural norms. They may be transgressive but never unnatural. The colour of jambul is the colour of the handsome Ram, the handsome Krishna and the handsome Kama Devas of Jain mythology. That is why India is called Jambudvipa, a reminder of male beauty and of female desire.

Devdutt Pattanaik

9

Ambitious Brides

*Men repay their debts to ancestors when wives become
mothers. Unless they repay their debts as husbands
there is no liberation for them.*

Once upon a time there was a woman who wanted her husband to pay her more attention than the rituals he was performing. Her name was Lopamudra. Her husband's name was Agastya. Her story is told in the Rig Veda, which is over 3000 years old. A thousand years later, by the time of the composition of the Mahabharata, the story changed dramatically. Agastya wanted Lopamudra to be the mother of his children, and she demanded compensation.

The Mahabharata and the Ramayana were epics composed in response to the Buddhist, Jain and other hermit challenges to Vedic rituals. Vedic rituals acknowledged human hunger and invoked gods and ancestors to satisfy that hunger. Buddhist and Jain monks saw the quest for food, to satisfy hunger, as the cause of misery. They sought to outgrow hunger and wanted contentment instead. This led to the rise of stories where the householder's choices were balanced with the hermit's choices. But both householder and hermit were men. What about the women?

In Vedic rituals, the *yagna-patni*, or the wife of the ritual performer, is an integral but invisible part of the ceremony. The hermit shunned women. The story of Agastya brought the attention back to women. Lopamudra wouldn't be a passive participant, simply responding to the choices of men.

As Agastya chose the hermit's life and sought to withdraw his senses from all material pleasures, he had a vision of his forefathers (pitr) hanging upside down over a bottomless pit, the hell of Put. They reminded him of his debt to them. He owed his life to the fathers who had come before him. He could repay this debt only by becoming a father himself. For that he needed a woman. But the woman wanted compensation. She wanted a house, income and attention, worthy of his children's mother.

Belief in rebirth is the distinguishing feature of Indian mythology, be it Buddhism, Jainism or Hinduism. Before Vedic times, the dead body was returned to the elements—buried in an urn or exposed to animals and birds or thrown into flowing rivers. Spirits of the dead lived with the living and could be summoned in special rituals by shamans who wore masks and went into trances. This practice continues in many folk and tribal traditions.

Vedic priests recommended burning the body and throwing the bones into rivers, to enable rebirth.

Special rituals were conducted to turn a ghost (pret) into a forefather (pitr), capable of being reborn. The dead who did not receive this final (*shraadh*) rite of passage (*samskara*) would stay back and haunt the living as poltergeists (*bhoot*), who trouble the living, and ghouls (*pisacha*), who trouble the dead.

A son has to perform suitable rituals for the dead, and also father children, preferably sons, to escape the terrible hell called Put. *Putra* and *putri*, Sanskrit words for son and daughter, are beings who rescue their parents from the hell of Put, reserved for those who did not fulfil their biological obligations. A son thus born has three debts to repay:

- Debt to forefathers, who gave us life, repaid by father's sons in turn.

- Debt to sages, who remembered and transmitted the Veda from earlier generations, repaid by learning and transmitting the Veda to the next generation.

- Debt to gods, who feed us, repaid by feeding them in turn.

Agastya was thus pressurized to marry. That was why he approached a king and asked for his daughter Lopamudra's hand in marriage. In these stories, the woman exists only to produce babies, only to help the man repay his debt to his ancestors. She liberates him from a huge debt, which is why the Hindu marriage is called kalyan even today—that which brings auspiciousness (mangala) into the man's life. Mangala is the experience of home, of love, of care, that comes with a woman. With her by his side, with the promise of the next generation, the man has the moral right to earn wealth and gather property. Once the debt is paid, however, the man is no longer obliged to stay with his wife.

- Rishi Kardama left his wife, Devahuti, after she bore him a son called Kapila.
- Jaratkaru left his wife after she bore their son Astika.
- The Buddha and the Tirthankaras left their families after fulfilling their social role as sons, fathers and brothers.

The wives were left to fend for themselves. But not all wives.

When Agastya told Lopamudra that he wanted her to bear his children, so he could repay his debt to his ancestors, she told him to compensate her adequately. He had to build her a beautiful house and provide enough resources for her and her children to live in comfort. So Agastya was forced to travel, help kings and gods, kill demons, and earn enough wealth to satisfy Lopamudra. He realized that to be truly liberated, he could not just repay his debt to his ancestors by incurring another debt. A husband's debt to his wife has to also be repaid.

By this story, the woman is not mere chattel. She is a partner in a network of exchange.

As many men pursued the monastic paths, stories were told to remind hermits that they had obligations to fulfil and debts to repay, before leaving the household. Women, therefore, play a prominent role in the epics, in contrast to earlier Vedic literature.

When Kaushalya was unable to bear him a child, Dashrath asked King Ashwapati for the hand of his daughter, Kaikeyi, in marriage. It had been foretold that she would be the mother of a great son. Kaikeyi married Dashrath on the assurance that her son would be king. Later, after a third marriage, Dashrath still had no children and was forced to admit that he was the problem. He conducted a Vedic ceremony at the end of which his three wives gave him four sons. But when he declared Ram, his eldest son born of his eldest queen, as his heir,

Kaikeyi got upset. She demanded her son be king. Promises made had to be kept.

In the Valmiki Ramayana, Kaikeyi comes across as being ambitious and disruptive and selfish, for simply asking what is owed to her. No one likes a debt-collector. In the Jain Ramayana, Kaikeyi feared her son Bharata would become a Jain monk. To prevent this from happening, Ram decided to go to the forest instead. It feels as if Ram was tricked into becoming a hermit so that Kaikeyi's son could be king.

In the Buddhist Ramayana, Ram was told to go to the forest as his father feared that his second wife would kill the heir apparent. The father was told by astrologers that he would die after twelve years, so Ram was told to survive in the forest and return to the palace after twelve years to claim his crown. Here it is suggested once again that men are pushed into monkhood as a result of palace politics and the machinations of ambitious women.

As in the Ramayana, in the Mahabharata it is women who push the plot forward by their desires and ambitions. Desires and ambitions of women are thus presented as the cause of male suffering.

King Shantanu fell in love with Ganga, the river goddess, and wanted to marry her. She agreed on one condition that he would never stop her from doing whatever she wanted to after marriage. She killed all the babies they bore. She agreed to be his wife, not his children's mother. As a goddess she knew her babies were actually cursed gods, forced to endure human life briefly. Shantanu did not know that. He wanted a wife, as well as a mother for his children. He stopped her from killing their eighth child. So Ganga left. She valued her freedom too much.

A free woman is thus compared to a river that does not like dams and canals, built by kings, to control her flow. Ganga's force is seen as disruptive, and so in art, she is often shown tamed in the matted hair of Shiva. She is the force of desire, who needs to be restrained by hermits, by matrimony and maternity. She is willing to sacrifice her freedom provided she gets something in return. She seeks a fair trade, like Harappan merchants, and like Vedic men who trade with gods, ancestors and sages.

After Ganga, Shantanu married a fisherwoman called Satyavati. But Satyavati too had conditions. She agreed to marry Shantanu only if he assured her that her children would be his heirs. In other words, he would pass on his throne and his crown to her sons and not to his sons born of his earlier marriage to Ganga.

Satyavati's ambition comes from a childhood wound, when she is denied her status as a princess.

Satyavati and her twin brother were found in the belly of a fish. The fisherfolk took the babies to the local king who adopted the boy but not the girl. So the brother became king while the sister became a boatwoman, ferrying people across the river. She was determined to become the wife of a king and then the mother of a king. To that end she agreed to bear a sage called Parasara a son called Vyasa, provided he replaced her body's fishy odour with a fragrant pheromone. This fragrant body got her the attention of King Shantanu, but she agreed to marry him only if he declared her future sons heirs to his throne.

Satyavati, spurned by her father who preferred a son, was an ambitious woman who demanded fair trade. She helped Rishi Parasara repay his debt to his ancestors only when he agreed to give her a fragrant body. She would satisfy Shantanu's lust only if he gave his kingdom to her children, thus making her mother of kings. She was not content being a king's mistress. She wanted to reclaim the royal status denied to her. Ambition is not just the arena of men.

Vedic men were under pressure to produce sons to please forefathers and gods. They needed wives. The women were not willing to see motherhood as their duty. They demanded a service fee, like a 'dakshina' given as tuition fee to the tutor in exchange for knowledge. This is evident in the different types of marriage described in later dharma-shastra literature:

1. In the way of Brahma (creator), the father gives his daughter to a man who approaches him.

2. In the way of prajapati (patriarch), the father gives his daughter to a man that he seeks out.

3. In the way of rishi (sage), the father gives his daughter to a forest-dwelling hermit, along with a bull and cow to establish a home.

4. In the way of deva (gods), the father gives his daughter to a man who works for him.

5. In the way of gandharva (celestial musician), the man seduces the woman.

6. In the way of asura (subterranean demon), the man buys the woman for a treasure.

7. In the way of rakshasa (raiding barbarian), the man abducts the woman.

8. In the way of pisacha (ghost), the man rapes the woman and forces her to bear his child.

The Vedic commentators preferred the first four over the last four marriage practices. The first four favoured the men; the last four reminded the men that women were in high demand and had rivals to contend with. The first four is the buyer's market, giving rise to gifts and dowries; the last four is the seller's market, giving rise to raids and thefts.

In dharma-shastra, there was great anxiety about not fathering sons. So, innovative laws were created to enable a man to be a father.

▪ A man is the father of the children of his wife, born before or after marriage. He can adopt children she bears with other men. This was how Vichitra, the younger son of Satyavati, became a father even after death. A suitable man was sent to his widows.

▪ Impotent and sterile men can allow their wives to go to other men and have children by them. This was how Pandu became the father of the five Pandavas. His two wives invoked five different gods.

In one folk tale, from the Kathasaritsagar, a king was about to make his annual offering to his ancestors when three hands sprang up from the waters to accept the pinda (ball of mashed rice meant for forefathers). These are identified as:

- The hand of the man who married his mother.
- The hand of the man who made his mother pregnant.
- The hand of the man who adopted him.

Who is the real father? Was Shakuntala's father Vishwamitra, the man who made Menaka pregnant, or Kanva, the man who raised her? No one really bothers with this question. But when it comes to Pandavas, in the Mahabharata, this becomes an important issue, as it deals with inheritance of property.

- The Vedic gods were the biological fathers of Pandavas.
- Devavrata–Bhisma was the foster father of the Pandavas.
- Pandu was the man who married the mother of Pandavas. This gave Pandavas legal rights over Pandu's crown. This made them rivals to the Kauravas.

In the Mahabharata, Devavrata was the last of the Kuru bloodline. But he vowed never to marry or father children to ensure only Satyavati's sons inherited his father's kingdom. In Jain versions, it is suggested that he even castrated himself so there was no doubt. This was why he was called Bhisma, the one who took the terrible vow.

Why terrible? Because he would never repay his debt to his ancestors and so would rot in Put forever, unable to be reborn. To protect his son, Shantanu gave Devavrata the boon to choose the time of his death. Devavrata let himself die only after the winter solstice, in the brighter half of the year, so he did not face the pitr, who come towards earth during the dark half of the year.

Basically, the Mahabharata is telling men they will suffer terribly if they do not father children. They need wives. And wives need to be treated with respect. Or at least adequately compensated, a practice started by Lopamudra.

10

She Who Said No

*Mithuna images from railings of a Buddhist stupa
showing a happy couple.*

The Ramayana is Hinduism's most popular epic. It is the story of Ram. But it is incomplete without Ram's wife, Sita, who plays a pivotal role in the narrative. It is common to project Sita as a tragic figure, a victim, a demure wife, who follows her husband to the jungle, only to find that she is being thrown out of the palace by him. But as one engages with her story, it emerges she is a woman with agency, who makes choices, and is witness to the ethical and moral dilemmas imposed by men, on men, in a patriarchal world.

There are as many ways of looking at Sita as there are of looking at the Ramayana.

- In nationalistic reading of the epic, Sita embodies all things Indian that have been, for the past 1000 years, taken away by Islamic, Christian and Marxist invaders. This is why on Hindutva posters Ram appears alone, in an aggressive stance, bearing a bow, ankles deep in the sea, while Hanuman's face reflects great fury.

- In feminist reading of the epic, Ram embodies Hindu patriarchy. He abandoned Sita, his faithful and dutiful wife, following public gossip about her character, even though she went through a fire trial to prove her purity. He also permitted the mutilation of Surpanakha, a forest woman who demanded sexual intimacy with him.

- In the Adbhuta Ramayana, a Tantrik retelling from the fifteenth century, i.e. five centuries ago, Sita took the form of a fierce goddess and killed a demon who attacked Ayodhya. He was ten times more powerful than Ravana, with 100 heads. Sita thus demonstrated to all that she was quite capable of protecting herself. That she let Ram defeat Ravana to establish his glory on earth.

- In the Valmiki Ramayana, the oldest narration, dated to 300 BC (2300 years ago), Ram and Sita were lovers, doomed to never be together because of social obligations (dharma) and their natural repercussions (karma). The epic began with Valmiki witnessing a hunter shoot down a bird, whose mate wailed piteously. An angry Valmiki cursed the hunter. The curse took the form of a poem. Valmiki realized how beautiful things could emerge from tragic events. And tragic events are the inevitable and inescapable consequences of duty: a hunter's job is to hunt. Dharma thus results in dharma-sankat (ethical and

Devdutt Pattanaik

moral dilemmas). Likewise, a king's job is to follow royal rules, which often come in the way of being a good husband, as in the case of Ram.

Ram is not a typical hero with ordinary human emotions, as in a Shakespeare play. He is Vishnu on earth. Vishnu is God: immortal, unfettered by space and time, full of wisdom. However, when God walks on earth, he is mortal, bound by rules of space and time. He has to perform the role determined by his social role. In other words, he has to be an avatar.

- If born as an animal, he has to behave like one.

- If born as a human, he has to behave as one.

- If born a prince, he is bound by royal rules.

- If born a cowherd, he has the freedom of a commoner.

Each of Vishnu's descents is meant to rescue the earth being plundered by insecure humans. That is why Vishnu is called the preserver. His story on earth as Ram is narrated in the Ramayana; his story as Krishna is narrated in the Mahabharata.

The Ramayana and the Mahabharata are called *itihasa*. While in Hindi the word means history, in Sanskrit it means a tale that is witnessed by the storyteller. Valmiki is witness to events in the Ramayana and Vyasa is witness to events in the Mahabharata. An itihasa is differentiated from a Purana, which are stories of gods that sages have not witnessed. The story of Vishnu comes from a Purana.

The Ramayana describes events of Ram avatar that occurred in the Treta Yuga, the second of the four quarters of the world's lifecycle. Here Vishnu is the eldest son of a royal family. The Mahabharata describes events that occurred in the Dvapara Yuga, the third quarter. Here Vishnu is Krishna, the youngest son of a cowherd family. We are currently in the fourth and final quarter, the Kali Yuga, in which the Buddha and Mahavira were born, who propagated the monastic path. It all starts and ends with pralaya — the flood of doom, into which all things dissolve, and from which all things emerge in Krita Yuga, the first quarter.

- For the nationalists who insist that mythology is history, the last flood of doom was the Ice Age, and events in the Ramayana took place around 7000 BC (9000 years ago). This is based on disputed astronomical information in the manuscripts, despite absence of any archaeological evidence.

Devdutt Pattanaik

- For historians who value evidence the story of the Ramayana evokes the early phase of the Vedic culture that thrived in the Gangetic plains between 1000 BC and 500 BC, before the establishment of southern trading routes and before the rise of monastic orders such as Buddhism and Jainism. The story, however, was put down in writing much later, between the Mauryan and the Gupta Empire, i.e. between 300 BC and 300 AD, so around 2000 years ago.

The story of Ram is also found in Jain and Buddhist literature. Most Jain Tirthankaras, and even the Buddha, descend from the Ikshvaku clan to which Ram belongs. Their stories come from the Gangetic river basin.

- In Jain literature, Ram was a special being called Baladeva, not an avatar of Vishnu. Here, waters rose to threaten the world when Sita did the fire trial to prove her fidelity, after being released from her captivity in Lanka. Sita also became a Jain nun.

- In Buddhist Dasharatha Jataka, the Buddha in his past life was Ram-Pandita but his story has nothing to do with Sita's abduction. It is about a prince who kept his word, at all costs. In the Shambuka Jataka, the Buddha-to-be admonished his son for abandoning his wife, who stood by him through misfortune, which alludes to the Ramayana theme.

In Jain and Buddhist lore, kings abandon their wives and go to the forest, in pursuit of spiritual wisdom. By contrast, in both Hindu epics, i.e. the Ramayana and the Mahabharata, palace politics forces kings to take refuge in the forest. They return wiser.

What is most remarkable about the Ramayana is that it is the only story in Hindu mythology where the male protagonist is valorized for being faithful to his wife and given the title of *ekam-patni-vrata*. Yet, he abandons his wife. This aspect of the epic rattles everyone, as people are torn between their loyalty to Ram, the Hindu god and Hindutva icon, and their feminist ideals. Why did the composer of the tale complicate his own story by showing his central character in poor light? Is that a code for something deeper?

As per Hindu mythology, Ram predates the Buddha. As per historians, the oldest manuscripts of the Ramayana were written after the Buddha preached his doctrine (dhamma). Brahmins recast an old oral story of a great king called Ram to establish the concept of a royal sage (tapasvi-raja), who neither feared suffering nor royal challenges, as the Buddha did.

Devdutt Pattanaik

We know very little about the Buddha's wife, Yashodhara, from Buddhist lore, but we know a lot more about Sita from the Ramayana.

Sita was found in a furrow by Janaka, the king of Videha. She was strong enough to pick up Shiva's bow, so it was decided that only a man who could string Shiva's bow would be allowed to marry her. Many tried but failed. Ram, the eldest son of King Dashrath of Ayodhya, broke the bow while trying to string it and won Sita's hand in marriage. Soon after her arrival in Ayodhya, there were preparations for Ram's coronation. But then she learnt that Ram had been asked by his father to go to the forest and live there for fourteen years, as a hermit, and let his younger brother, Bharat, be crowned king instead. Ram agreed without resistance. However, his brother Lakshman decided to join him in the forest. So did Sita. Ram, Sita and Lakshman survived the forest in great hardship, fighting demons and visiting hermits. In the final year of exile, Sita was abducted by a rakshasa king called Ravana. Ram rescued her, but the rescue was not easy. He needed the help of monkeys (*vanar*), who built a bridge to the island kingdom of Ravana. After a fierce battle, Ram defeated Ravana and liberated Sita. Together they returned home to Ayodhya.

This should have been a happy ending. But the Ramayana is not the tale of a hero's triumph or tragedy, it is the biography of Ram and Sita, from their birth to their death. So the story continues.

When Sita returned to Ayodhya, she became the subject of great gossip. Ram, who was now the king, learnt how people were questioning Sita's fidelity. He feared his royal reputation would be stained, so he asked Lakshman to abandon Sita in the forest. There Sita gave birth to Ram's children. In the final chapter of the story, Ram is united with his sons, but Sita refuses to join him on his throne and descends into the earth, whence she came. Unable to bear this separation, a heartbroken Ram decides to give up his life in the Sarayu River.

The Ramayana has a tragic ending. Many argue that the original Ramayana ended with Ram's triumph and the tragic last chapter was added later. But located in the Ramayana are seeds that sprout in the Mahabharata. Karma links the two epics, makes them two chapters in a larger narrative of Vishnu.

- Ram, who ascended to Vaikuntha at the end of Treta Yuga, descends as Krishna, with the passage of time, in Dvapara Yuga.

- Women who desired Ram but were turned away are reborn as milkmaids who find delight in Krishna's company.

- Krishna marries Jambavati, the daughter of Jambavan, who served Ram and helped rescue Sita.

- Since Ram supported Sugriva, son of the sun god Surya, against Vali, son of the rain god Indra, Krishna is obliged to balance the scale by supporting Arjuna, son of Indra, against Karna, son of Surya.

The Ramayana is not the story of a son, brother, husband or father, even though Ram plays all these roles. It is the story of an ideal king, who values royal reputation over everything else. This is why he fulfils the king's wishes unconditionally, kills demons in the forest to protect sages and fights the strong who abuse the weak.

Nationalists say he is the ideal man, Purushottama. Feminists beg to differ. How can a man who abandoned his pregnant wife be ideal? Both overlook the adjective *maryada*. Ram is Maryada Purushottama (he who follows rules, he who is steadfast) and needs to be distinguished from Krishna, who is Leela Purushottama (he who plays games, he who bends and breaks rules).

- As the eldest son of a royal family, Ram is obliged to follow rules. His antagonist is Ravana, also a king, who does not care for rules and uses his power to dominate the weak.

- As the youngest adopted son of a cowherd family, Krishna is free to bend rules. His antagonist is Indra, Kamsa, Jarasandha and Duryodhan, kings who use trickery to twist rules and exploit the weak.

Both are forms of Vishnu, the infinite divine, existing in two different contexts. Both institute dharma on earth. Dharma is different from rules. Dharma is about the spirit of the law, not letter of the law. Laws exist to protect the powerless from the powerful. As king, Ram is expected to follow the rules, without questioning them. But when kings misuse the rules, you need a Krishna to outsmart the tricksters. Ram cannot do what Krishna does; they are limited by their contexts.

In Western mythology, rules play a key role. God makes the rules, communicated through angels and prophets, that humans have to follow. From time to time, God changes the rules. Only God can change the rules. Muslims believe the last set of rules were given to Muhammad. Jews and Christians disagree. But all of them agree that following God's rule gets you to heaven while breaking God's rule casts you in hell, though God is merciful and will forgive if you repent.

Western mythology ignores the dichotomy between nature and culture, which is the hallmark of Vedic thought.

- In nature (*prakriti*), the strong consume the weak. It is the world of food chain and pecking orders, of domination, of territoriality, of strength and cunning, where alphas rule, where might is right and where all that matters is survival.

- In culture (*sanskriti*), kings exist to protect the weak. To help the helpless is dharma. But with dharma comes dharma-sankat, or moral and ethical dilemmas. For the act of consumption is violent. To protect the meek, the king needs resources. To satisfy the mighty, the king needs resources. To be in charge, the king needs resources. The accumulation of resource involves violence.

The need to judge the Ramayana comes from cultures that believe in Judgement Day and seek justice. Middle Eastern mythologies do not talk about rebirth. They believe in one life; hence value is placed on living this life the right way. There is no second chance. Indian mythology talks about karma — that actions yield reactions. The present is a reaction to the past and the future is a reaction to the present. And that karma carries forward into future lives. Without factoring in rebirth and karma, the Ramayana cannot be understood.

As a mortal, Ram is bound by karmic laws, even when he upholds dharma. He pays the price for his actions:

- When Lakshman mutilates Surpanakha, justifying his actions on the grounds that the woman did not respect Ram's consent, he sets in motion a series of reactions that culminates in the abduction of Sita.

- When Ram kills Vali, who oppresses his weak brother Sugriva, Ram is cursed by Vali's widow, Tara, that he will never experience conjugal joy.

- When Ram kills Ravana, who grabs other people's wives with alacrity, Ram is cursed by Ravana's widow, Mandodari, that he will never experience conjugal joy.

In stories, karma manifests as curses and boons. Ram is cursed and so circumstances force him to abandon Sita. Though a king, though a divine being, he is helpless before karma. Sita should not be abandoned. She is innocent; she even gives evidence of her purity, but still she is abandoned. Does Ram doubt her? No, he does not; that is why he never remarries; that is why he puts an effigy of gold to represent her in domestic rituals. Gold is a metaphor for purity.

Devdutt Pattanaik

People often argue that Sita was innocent, so she should not have been abandoned. What if she was not innocent? Should a woman be abandoned then? In the story of Ahalya, who was cursed to turn into stone by her husband, who found her in the arms of Indra, nobody is sure if Ahalya was guilty or innocent. Still, Ram's teacher, Vishwamitra, told Ram to forgive her, liberate her and restore her to her husband. Great kings give the benefit of doubt, they purify the impure and uplift the fallen. Purity is a subjective concept. Reputation is also a subjective concept. Kings care for reputation above all else. They need to be trusted by a people. They cannot be seen as favouring family under any circumstances.

Consent is a key theme in dharma. People highlight obligations as a key theme of dharma and ignore the role of consent. In the forest, there are no obligations or consent. Animals grab and take what they want. The mighty overpowers the meek. In the world of dharma, such force is frowned upon. The mighty have obligations; the meek have consent. Ram and his family embody dharma. Ravana and his family prefer the jungle way and so embody adharma. Between them are the monkeys, the vanar, struggling with animal instinct and human potential.

- Ram lives to uphold royal values; Ravana chooses to indulge his passions.

- The vanar king Sugriva struggles with obligations; his brother, Vali, chooses to be alpha.

- Surpanakha does not care for Ram's consent; Ravana does not care for Sita's consent.

What about Sita's consent? When you read the Ramayana carefully you realize Sita is constantly making choices. Her choices determine the direction of the story.

In the final chapter, when Ram abandoned Sita, he did it in a very uncharacteristic way. Ram was someone who always followed the rules. Yet, when it was time to abandon Sita, he did it through deceit. Sita wanted to visit the forest to bathe in the river. Ram told Lakshman to take her where she wanted to go and not bring her back. He did not tell Sita that he had planned to abandon her. She was simply abandoned in the forest. And that's a shocking thing to happen to any person, let alone a pregnant woman. Lakshman took Sita to the forest and then told her that Ram had abandoned her. She was free to go wherever she wants to. But she was not welcome at the palace in Ayodhya. We are told Sita was heartbroken.

So, why did Ram not tell Sita about his decision? The reason is rather simple. Every time Ram told Sita to do something, she said no.

When Ram was going into the forest for his fourteen-year exile, he told Sita to stay back and live in the palace in Ayodhya. Sita said no, she would go too. 'I will be with you every step of the way.' This was the first time she made a choice. Later, Sita was told not to cross the line known as Lakshman Rekha. It was the line drawn around their hut by Lakshman, for her own protection. Yet, Sita crossed the line. Not because she wanted to disobey Lakshman, but because she felt feeding a hungry man was more important than her security. Unfortunately for her, the man outside her hut, begging for food, was not a hungry man; it was Ravana, a demon in disguise. This was the second time she made a choice. Still later, when Sita was in Lanka, she was visited by Hanuman. He was the great monkey general who could fly through the air and was so strong that he could carry mountains. Hanuman asked Sita to hop on his back so that he could take her back to her husband. Once again Sita said no because she wanted Ram to rescue her. She wanted Ram to defeat Ravana so that no one could say that Ram could not protect his wife. Sita was very concerned about Ram's reputation as a king. This was the third time she made a choice. Finally, after Ravana had been defeated and Ram finally met Sita at Lanka, he told her, 'I cannot take you back to Ayodhya. The people of Ayodhya will not accept you, as you have stayed in another man's house.' Sita once again said no. 'I will come back to you. I will come back with you to Ayodhya, I will stand by you, even if people gossip about me.' This was the fourth time she made a choice.

Perhaps that was why Ram did not tell Sita. When he decided to abandon her, he knew she would argue and get her way. She would say no, she would defy him. Her father, Janaka, was an intellectual, so she was well versed in the art of debate. Ram was simply the king who followed the rules of the land. He knew how to submit to the law and obey the rules. He did not know how to defy the system and argue the way Sita did, like a lawyer.

In the final chapter, Sita once again said no. Sita returned Ram's children to him. Ram then told Sita that the people of Ayodhya had realized that she had been faithful to him all her life in thought and deed. 'So please return to Ayodhya,' he said. But Sita refused and returned to her mother's home, under the earth. This was her fifth and final choice.

Devdutt Pattanaik

Sita did not choose everything in her life. Sita's marriage was not her choice. It was not a love marriage. She did not choose Ram to be her husband. She was given to Ram, like a trophy, because he broke Shiva's bow. Her union with Ram was not her choice; her separation from him was not her choice either.

Sita knew that life is a combination of circumstances that we do not choose and responses that we do choose. She was, after all, the daughter of Janaka, a king closely linked with the Upanishad, Vedic texts that introduced the idea of karma. Circumstances, over which we have no control, is karma, shaped by our past choices. Choice, over which we have control, is also karma, as it shapes our future circumstances.

If we look at Sita, without reducing her to a victim, we realize that she, like many other women in ancient lore, took decisions, sometimes right, sometimes wrong. Each choice had consequences, some good, some bad. These were accepted with grace. No one was blamed. Liberty is not a new concept. It has always been around. And it always comes at a price.

11

Documentation of Descent

The image of seven nameless wild goddesses (yoginis?) with one man (lover, brother, son?) is a popular theme for silver talismans found in rural areas across India.

Draupadi seems more a modern feminist icon than Sita.

- Draupadi had five husbands, and she demanded the murder of the men who abused her, refusing to tie her hair until it was washed in their blood.

- Sita remained faithful to her husband even when she was wrongfully accused of infidelity and abandoned in the forest despite undergoing a fire trial to prove her innocence. Sita never screamed. She endured her humiliation silently.

However, in the end, it is Sita's children who become kings, not Draupadi's. Draupadi's children are slain in their sleep, victims of vendetta.

The story of Draupadi, and of women in the epic Mahabharata, reveals the gradual descent in the status of women. They have far lesser consent and agency than Sita. This may be the reason why, mythologically speaking, Sita belongs to an earlier, brighter age, the Treta Yuga, while Draupadi belongs to the Dvapara Yuga, the age before the current dark Kali Yuga.

In the Ramayana, it is clear that the eldest son Ram should be king. There is a conflict because his father had promised the throne to the son that his second wife would bear him and because his father had promised to fulfil the wishes of his second wife. The conflict emerges between the law of the land and the king's commitment to the queen.

In the Mahabharata, the hundred Kauravas argue that the five Pandavas are not of royal bloodline; Pandu was not their biological father. But then the Kauravas are told that their father Dhritarashtra, is also not of royal bloodline. Dhritarashtra's father, Vichitravirya, had died childless. Pandu and Dhritarashtra were products of levirate; their widowed mothers were forced to go to a sage and produce heirs for the dead king. The last of the royal bloodline was Vichitravirya's elder brother, Bhisma, who had taken the vow of celibacy. The conflict in the Mahabharata is thus clearly about succession. And it is clear bloodline threads through men, not women.

This is what happens in the first generation.

King Shantanu falls in love, first with Ganga who is the river goddess, and then with Satyavati a fisherwoman. Each woman demanded compensation before they agreed to marry him. Ganga told Shantanu that he should never question her actions after marriage. Satyavati told Shantanu that her sons should be sole inheritors of his property. Only when Shantanu agreed to these conditions, the women decided to marry him.

This is what happens in the second generation.

Amba and Ambika were princesses of Kashi. On Satyavati's orders, they were abducted and forced to marry Satyavati's son, Vichitravirya, who unfortunately died before he could make either of them pregnant. The two princesses were then forced by their mother-in-law to go to Vyasa and have children by him. Those children legally belonged to the royal household. In this story, the sisters had no control over their bodies. They resisted the levirate marriage. They did not want to go to a strange man. As a result, we are told, Amba's son Dhritarashtra was born blind, while Ambika's son Pandu was born a weakling, probably impotent, attributed to a curse.

This is what happens in the third generation.

Gandhari did not realize until her wedding night that her husband Dhritarashtra was blind. She blindfolded herself. She bore her husband a hundred mediocre sons, forcing them out of her womb by striking her belly with an iron bar on learning that her rival, Kunti, had borne her first son, the first grandchild of the royal household. Kunti chose to marry Pandu. But there were rumours that she had had a child before marriage; this made her an unsuitable bride. So, a more suitable Madri was given to Pandu. Pandu could not make either of his wives pregnant, owing to a curse. During a deer hunt, he accidentally killed a forest-dweller who was making love to his wife. And so was told he would die the instant he touched any woman. In shame, Pandu decided to leave the palace and live in the forest, thereby relinquishing his claim to the throne. There he was told that men like him could have children through the system of levirate. If he permitted his wives, they could go to other men and have children by them, whom he could adopt. Pandu granted this permission and his two wives invoked gods, using a magical power that Kunti had. Pandu adopted the three sons of Kunti and two sons of Madri, who became known as the five talented Pandavas. Pandu died when he could not resist touching the attractive Madri. An ashamed Madri killed herself on his funeral pyre, leaving Kunti to raise the five children and secure their inheritance.

This happens in the fourth generation.

Arjuna, the archer son of Pandu, was able to win an archery competition. The trophy was Draupadi, daughter of King Drupada of Panchala. His mother forced Arjun to share his trophy—wife with his four brothers. Before Draupadi, Bhima had married Hidimba, a rakshasa woman, and had a son by her, Ghatotkacha. However, for Kunti, Hidimba was an unsuitable wife, a forest-dwelling rakshasa, who could not secure the Pandava inheritance. Draupadi, daughter of a king, gave the Pandavas a leverage. With Drupada as their father-in-law, the Pandavas were able to force the Kurus to divide the family land and give them their share of the property.

With each generation we see a gradual deterioration in the status of women.

- Ganga and Satyavati controlled their bodies and demanded compensation from their husbands. Ganga focused on her freedom. Satyavati was concerned about her status, as wife and mother.

- Amba and Ambalika had no agency; they were reduced to baby-making machines, by their mother-in-law. Ambika and Ambalika were forced to go to a sage. They resisted, so their children were born with disabilities. A warning to future generations of wives.

- Gandhari, Kunti and Madri are rivals as they strive to bear heirs for the royal family. Gandhari had no idea that her husband is born blind. Kunti is supplemented by Madri, of unstained reputation, as Kunti had had a child before marriage. Both wives of Pandu go to other men to bear children for their husbands. Gandhari envied Kunti who bore the firstborn of the clan. Kunti envied Madri, who cleverly invoked twin gods, hence two sons, with just one mantra. Fearing Madri would end up with more children, Kunti, who had borne three sons through three gods, did not let Madri invoke any more gods. Kunti would not let the prettier and purer Madri become the dominant wife too.

- Gandhari did not choose her husband. A blind king was chosen for her. Draupadi did not choose five husbands. She was a trophy at an archery competition, and she was shared by five brothers. And like the kingdom they shared, the Pandava brothers wagered Draupadi in a gambling match and lost her to the Kauravas, who abused her in public. They dragged her by the hair out of the inner chambers and attempted to disrobe her in public. Draupadi was forced to ask the question, 'Do men who lose themselves in a gambling match have the right to gamble their wives?' And she was told quite bluntly, 'As property of the husband, she was already a slave when her five husbands became slaves.'

All these stories are part of the Mahabharata's first chapter, the Adi Parva. They explain the origin of patriarchy and link it with inheritance. Here we also see women participating in the emerging social structure that strips women of agency. Satyavati ordered the abduction and eventual levirate of her daughters-in-law. Kunti insisted Hidimba be left behind in the forest and Draupadi be shared by her five sons. And no man came to the rescue of Draupadi as she was wagered in a game of dice and abused by those who won the gambling match.

The idea of polyandry (woman marrying many men) rattles many in modern times, even those who feel polygyny (man marrying many woman) is normal.

- Polyandry prevents division of property, as all children belong to the common wife. Marisha married the Pracheta brothers and bore them Daksha, the patriarch.

- Polygyny, by contrast, results in property disputes and division of property, between half-brothers. This is clearly evident in the Ramayana where Kaikeyi wants her son to be king.

However, in societies with high infant mortality and high maternal mortality, polygamy ensures the survival of a tribe, not polyandry. Hence polygamy is encouraged over polyandry. Marriage in the

Mahabharata is all about enabling the transmission of property through legitimate heirs. No one asks why Dashrath has three wives, but everyone wonders why Draupadi has five husbands. It is seen as a burden, or even a punishment. Stories are told to explain Draupadi's situation.

In her previous life, Draupadi was Nalanyani who pestered her husband so much for pleasure that he cursed her that she would have many husbands to satisfy her lust. Draupadi asked Shiva for five great capabilities in one husband, but Shiva misheard and ended up giving her five husbands each with one great capability. Every Pandava had been once an Indra, and since there is only one Sachi for every Indra, the five Pandavas were given a common wife on earth, who was Sachi reborn. Draupadi was told the story of Tilotamma, over whom two brothers fought and killed each other. To prevent the five Pandavas fighting each other, Draupadi sets a rule by which she is wife to only one brother each year. They take turns sequentially, one year at a time. That way every husband knew they were the father of the child she bore that year.

But while Draupadi was intimate with each of her five husbands after a gap of five years, her husbands, who had many wives, carried no such burden. They could visit anyone anytime.

Arjun once accidentally interrupted the lovemaking of Yudhishthira and Draupadi. So he was punished and asked to stay away from the palace for twelve years, losing three opportunities to be with Draupadi. During this exile, he married three women: Ulupi, Chitrangada and Subhadra. Each of them bore him sons: Iravan, Babruvahan and Abhimanyu.

The punishment turned into some kind of sexual compensation. The Mahabharata thus subtly reminds us that one woman having many husbands is not the same as one man having many wives. Draupadi bears five children to five men in five years. Arjuna fathers three sons in a single year.

The Mahabharata speaks of a time when marriage laws were fluid. There were no clear rules of fidelity. These may be stories before the origin of property or the concept of ownership. People sought virile and talented men to make the women in their household pregnant. Fidelity was not much of a concern.

Brihaspati wanted to make love to his sister-in-law Mamata, the wife of Utathya. But she stopped him, not because she found his desire inappropriate but because she was already pregnant. In fury, Brihaspati cursed Mamata that the child in her womb would be born blind. Thus was born Dirghatama, whose wife wanted to have many husbands and so abandoned him on a raft set adrift on a river. King Bali rescued

Dirghatama and requested him to make his queen, Sudeshna, pregnant. Dirghatama gave Sudeshna three sons, who went on to become kings of Anga, Vanga and Kalinga.

Kunti tells Pandu the story of Shvetaketu, who discovered his mother in the arms of another man and was alarmed when his father, Uddalaka, did not condemn it. So he insisted on imposing the laws of marriage and stripped women of agency. This is how marriage starts—to identify paternity. Fathers now could bequeath their property to their sons. Draupadi bears one son for each of her husbands. She is the mother of five sons. These sons can potentially split the Pandava kingdom into five parts. But that does not happen, as Draupadi's five sons are killed in the war against the hundred Kaurava brothers.

When she agreed to marry the five Pandava brothers, Draupadi had only one request. 'You will not get a woman into the house I live in. You all can have other wives, but they will not live under my roof.' But she was tricked by Arjuna, who brought a second wife into the house, Subhadra. Subhadra's only son, Abhimanyu, like Draupadi's five sons, is killed in the war at Kurukshetra. However, unlike Draupadi's sons, Subhadra's son leaves behind an unborn son. This is the only surviving male heir of the Pandava brothers, Parikshit.

Devdutt Pattanaik

What is even more remarkable in the great epic is the genealogy of Parikshit.

- His mother was Uttara, the daughter of Virata, of the Matsya kingdom, who was a descendant of Satyavati's brother. Satyavati and her brother were both found in the belly of a fish. The king of Matsya adopted the brother and let Satyavati be raised by fisherfolk. Through Uttara, Satyavati effectively became the ancestress of kings.

- His grandmother was Subhadra, of the Yadu clan. Long ago, Yayati gave his kingdom to his youngest son, Puru, rather than his eldest son, Yadu. From Puru came the Kuru clan to which the Kauravas and the Pandavas belong. Through Subhadra, Yadu's lineage reclaimed Kuru lands.

These complex genealogies reduce women to their biological function. They stop being people. They become chattel. Unlike the Ramayana, where we are constantly made aware of the love between Ram and Sita, in the Mahabharata, we get a sense that no one truly loves Draupadi.

In the Ramayana, Ravana saw Sita as Ram's property. By abducting her, he hurt Ram. But Ram saw Sita as an independent agent under his protection. He fought for her, not because she belonged to him, but because he was the king who was supposed to protect everyone in his care. Sita's autonomy is proven time and time again. When Ravana was killed and Sita was released from captivity, Ram informed her that as king he could not accept her as queen, as she won't be welcomed back into the royal household. So she should choose another husband. Sita, however, insisted on returning home to Ayodhya as Ram's wife, refusing to accept that the royal household would have a problem with her, especially after she did the fire trial to prove her fidelity. Things in the Mahabharata seem bleaker.

Draupadi's humiliation in the gambling hall, angered the gods. They shamed and terrified the Kaurava elders into letting the Pandava brothers reclaim their land. But as the five men were leaving the gambling hall, the Kaurava brothers taunted their male pride. 'Saved by a woman!' they chuckled. To restore their dignity, the Pandavas agreed to play one more match to win their lands back. But they lost and forfeited the right to their kingdom for thirteen years. For twelve years they lived in a forest, away from all settlements. In the final year, they went into hiding; if caught, they would have to go back into exile for another thirteen years.

During the exile, Draupadi was sexually assaulted twice. Each time, she realized how useless her husbands were. The first time it involves a family member.

In the early years of exile, Jayadhrata paid a visit to the Pandava camp. He was Dushala's husband, the only sister of the Kauravas. Finding Draupadi alone, he tried to convince her to come with him to his palace and live in comfort. When she expressed disgust at his suggestion and asked him to leave, he tried to take her by force. She was rescued by her husbands, in time. But they refused to punish Jayadhrata because he was their brother-in-law, and they did not want Dushala to become a widow. Her widowhood become additional cause of rift between them and the Kauravas.

The second assault happens during the final year, when the Pandavas live in hiding. Here, for the first time in India's epic tradition, there is an exploration of exploitative violence by elites against servants, slaves and service-providers.

In the final year of exile, the Pandavas hid as servants in the court of King Virata, Draupadi took the role of a hairdresser to the queen. The queen's brother-in-law, Kichaka, sexually harassed her. The queen ignored her complaints. Instead of coming to her rescue, Yudhishtira asked her to suffer silently. Discretion, he said, was the better part of valour. If Kichaka was killed, the world would know where the Pandavas were hiding and that would further complicate their already fragile situation. Arjuna agreed with his brother. A frustrated Draupadi finally manipulated and goaded Bhima to kill Kichaka anyway, much to Yudhishtira's irritation.

These stories leave us in no doubt that the Mahabharata documents the declining status of women. The unbound hair and the screams of Draupadi embody not power but helplessness of a privileged elite woman, abandoned by the very men who had promised to protect her.

12

Circles of Women

Divinity in Hinduism is expressed as union of God and Goddess.
Without either there is neither.

No conversation of Krishna today is complete without the mention of Radha. But Radha was never Mrs Krishna in the way that Sita was Mrs Ram. This prompts some puritans to present complex mystical explanations for their union.

We are conditioned to accept male and female relationships only within the framework of marriage. Radha challenged this framework, as she overshadowed Krishna's many wives, yet remained autonomous. Hermits abandon their wives in the pursuit of spiritual goals, kings reject wives because of their royal reputation, but here is a case of an ordinary woman, enjoying a man, being enjoyed by him, revelling in playfulness, unbound by law or convention, seeking nothing in exchange. She is her own person; her identity does not come from being a man's or god's mother, daughter, sister or wife.

Every year, at the height of summer, just before the summer solstice, in the coastal town of Puri, Odisha, three chariots leave the famous temple of Jagannath and travel north, up the road, to a garden temple. It's a grand ceremony known as the Rath Yatra or the chariot festival. The deities stay in the garden temple for nine days and return in time for the annual four-month sleep of Vishnu, which corresponds ritually to the four months of the monsoon rains.

During this stay in the garden temple, Goddess Lakshmi, left behind in the main temple, protests and demands her husband return from his sojourn with his siblings. Meanwhile, Jagannath takes the form of Krishna and engages in *raas-lila* (performance of sensory delight), a mysterious, mystical dance, where he plays the flute and milkmaids dance in a circular formation around him, in the forest, at night, enjoying the moonlight and the heady fragrance of flowers. Here Radha is the female protagonist.

In the local temple tradition of Puri, Jagannath is both *avatari* and avatar. As avatari, he is the immortal and timeless Vishnu. As avatar, he is mortal and bound by time. He becomes Vaman, the Brahmin; Ram, the king; and Krishna, the cowherd. Krishna's life is divided into two parts. A childhood surrounded by women who showered him with maternal, romantic and erotic love, and a youth surrounded by men, who were ambitious, petty, fragile and greedy. When Krishna left the village of women, he promised he would return. He never did.

The chariot festival is a ritual fulfilment of Krishna's promise. He returns to Gokul (the settlement of cowherds), which is also Vrindavan (the forest of fragrant basil) and Madhuban (the wood of sweet delight). For here lives Radha, Krishna's beloved. Their relationship is not bound by law. She is not his mother, daughter, sister or wife. It is a relationship that breaks all convention. She is older than him, married to another man, and his aunt, depending on which poetry one refers to.

She made her first appearance in literature only eight centuries ago, in the twelfth-century Sanskrit work, *Gita Govinda*, by Jayadeva. The song began with Krishna as a child terrified of the dark rain clouds in a forest of dark trees as the darkness of night approached. So his father, Nanda, told the older Radha to take him home. On the way, a secret unfolded, as the child became a man and the woman her lover. They made love in every bush and bower on the banks of the dark Yamuna.

It is evening, clouds are gathering in the sky,
the forest is dark with tamala trees,
and Krishna is afraid of the darkness of night.
Nandagopa asks Radha to take Krishna
home safely.
Victory to the love sports of Radha and Madhava
in the secrecy of every bush and bower
on the banks of Yamuna, on their way home.
Poet Jayadeva whose heart is the abode of

Goddess Saraswati, who is the chief devotee
at the lotus feet of Radha is writing this work
in which are included descriptions of the love
sports of Krishna.
If your mind revels in remembering Krishna
and if you are interested in the art of love
then listen to these sweet and tender verses
of Jayadeva's work.

This unconventional aspect of Radha's love for
Krishna is vociferously denied by twentieth-century
Krishna cults, all controlled by men. These elite men
also prefer to see Krishna as blue, rather than simply
dark-complexioned. They want to see Krishna as a
twice-born elite or *dvija*, even though Krishna is always
visualized either as a cowherd or as a charioteer. They
want to purify Krishna: make him otherworldly,
rising up towards the sky, even though Radha, like
the Yamuna River, flows down. They feel embarrassed
by the erotic longing for Krishna, emerging from
traditional poetry, that evokes the mood of sweetness
(*madhurya rasa*) and mood of delight (*shringara rasa*).
They eclipse these ideas by publicly proclaiming,
like Christian and Islamic missionaries, that God
is homophobic, or that God wants women to be
submissive to men.

The idea of Krishna first appeared in Indo–Greek coins as early as the second century BC (2200 years ago). His romantic and erotic side began only after the fifth century AD (1500 years ago). It played a key role in countering the monastic Buddhist and Jain orders and reimagining of Hinduism. The idea of Radha appears only around the twelfth century AD (800 years ago) as the feminine half of the divine is given a more central role. However, after the fifteenth century AD (500 years ago), it was downplayed. This was the Bhakti Age, or the age of devotion, when the only acceptable form of devotion, under the influence of Muslim rulers, was the one of Sufis—disembodied, formless, high and distant.

In Hinduism, divinity is embodied and formless, present everywhere, within everything as well as around everything, manifesting differently in different stages of realization, like seeds in different stages of germination. The deity and the devotee are on equal planes. So the devotee can even be a mother (like Yashoda to Krishna) or a friend (like Arjuna to

Krishna). As a milkmaid of Gokul, she can also be the demanding, quarrelsome, swooning lover.

The theme of an erotic hero, or god, who drives women wild is a repetitive theme in early Indian literature.

- In Jain lore, heroes such as Vasudeva, Jivaka and Brahmadatta were so handsome that wherever they went, women wanted to marry them. They won the hearts of women by defeating demons, winning martial competitions, impressing people with their song and dance, with their understanding of perfumes and fashion, and even with the use of wit. Balarama was so handsome that he turned his body towards a wall to meditate when he noticed that women, distracted by his beauty, had stopped doing their daily chores.

- Shiva's beauty made the wives of priests chase him, earning the wrath of their husbands who sent tigers, snakes and demons to attack Shiva.

- Ram's beauty made even hermits in the forest want him as their husband but since he had sworn fidelity to Sita, he promised to satisfy them in his next life as Krishna, when they would be reborn as women.

- Krishna's beauty made the wives of cowherds abandon their husbands and families at night and dance with him in the secret fragrant grove in the forest. Radha, as a character, appeared late in the description of this secret dalliance. There, on a full-moon night, Krishna, anointed with sandalwood paste and bedecked with forest flowers, made music with his flute. The milkmaids of the village, the gopikas, danced around him. They spent the night in joy, in each other's company. Before dawn, the women returned home. The men of the village had no idea what had happened, and the women were happy with their secret.

Krishna's love for milkmaids appears in earlier Sanskrit works like the Harivamsa and Vishnu Purana, dated around the sixth century. The circular dance is described in the Bhagavata Purana, dated around the tenth century. Radha appeared only in the twelfth century Sanskrit poetry of Jayadeva. Chaitanya mainstreamed the circular dance of Krishna and Radha, and the milkmaids in the sixteenth century. His followers discovered the original location of this story in Mathura, close to Delhi. The period that followed marked the rediscovery of Radha's love for Krishna by poets in the Mithila, Bengal and Odisha regions, in the seventeenth and eighteenth centuries. The poems, composed in local languages such as Maithili and Braj Bhasha, Bengali and Odia, revealed spiritual longings that defied convention in every possible way. They were simultaneously clandestine, erotic and devotional. Late Sanskrit works, such as the Brahmavaivarta, strove to sanitize everything by insisting Krishna and Radha were a celestial married couple, embodying primal spirit and primal matter, and their dance had deep spiritual meaning that was misunderstood by uninitiated souls—a common explanation for Tantrik symbols that embarrassed many.

So, we see a story transforming over time. In earlier works, Krishna was chased by married women, establishing him as a powerful erotic hero. The relationship was transgressive. Rules were being broken. Slowly, this intense erotic energy transformed into something occult, as the women danced in a circular arrangement, at night. With the arrival of Radha, a single woman took centre stage and became Krishna's equal, even dominant. But then, gradually, we find a downplaying of the eroticism, and a greater restraint in the language. Women were sidelined once more, by the patriarch and the hermit. Despite explicit miniature paintings produced in Rajput courts, we are told the relationship was not physical, it was emotional. It was *prema*, not *kama*. We are told Krishna was not taking pleasure from the women, he was giving them pleasure; he exhausted them but remained inexhaustible. She needed him, he did not need her or anyone, for he was the infinite limitless divine.

Devdutt Pattanaik

The circle of women around Krishna has precedence. We find several such circles of women in earlier traditions:

- The circle of women (the *ganika*) around the Buddha's stupa.
- The circle of women (the *nakshatra*) in the sky, around Chandra, the moon god.
- The circle of women (the yogini) on cremation grounds, around male Tantrik deities, such as Bhairava and Heruka.
- The circle of women (the apasara) on the walls of Jain and Hindu temples.

The circle of women first appeared around a Buddhist stupa, in Bhuteshwar, Mathura, dated to the second century AD (1800 years ago). The images found on the railings show bejewelled, confident and happy women, standing atop a misshapen yaksha image below galleries where stand a couple, probably donors. These single women are believed to be independent female hospitality providers (*ganika*) —

playful, beautiful, bejewelled, bold and confident. They embody the principle of pleasure. They face outwards, away from the mound where the relic of the Buddha is buried. We can speculate that they embody the world of temptations (bhoga), the cause of worldly suffering, that the Buddha wanted to shun.

In the Shiva Purana, composed around the fifth century AD (1500 years ago), we hear of another circle of women. This time in the sky. This is the circle of nakshatras. Nowadays, we divide the sky into twelve parts: the Zodiac or the Rashi. The concept of Zodiac came to India much later, about 2000 years ago with the Greeks, the Babylonians and the Persians. But before that, in the Vedic Age, and perhaps even in the Harappan Age, the sky was divided based on the constellations known as nakshatras.

There were twenty-seven such constellations, said to be daughters of Daksha Prajapati. All were given in marriage to the moon god, Chandra. However, Chandra had only one favourite—Rohini. So the other wives got upset and cursed Chandra that he would lose his lustre with the passage of time. As a result, the moon began to wane. To restore his lustre, he was asked by the gods to pray to Shiva. Shiva placed Chandra on his head, where the Ganga flowed. There Chandra's virility was restored. Having learnt his lesson, Chandra now visits each of his wives. He waxes as he moves closest to his favourite, Rohini, and wanes as he moves away from her. Then, he sits on Shiva's forehead, lets the Ganga water nourish him, just before and through the new moon, so that he can resume his journey of waxing and waning lustre.

This story draws attention to a very common Indian belief that pleasure grants women power but strips men of power. Bhoga is the cause of decay, degeneration, disease and death. This was why women were shunned by Buddhist and Jain monks. That is why, in the Buddhist stupa, the joyful women face outwards.

This idea of outward-facing circle of women reappears in many Jain and Hindu temples, built after the twelfth century (800 years ago). They are described as pleasure women and divine damsels (apsara). Sometimes they are even described as myriad manifestations of fortune (shri), power (shakti) and knowledge (vidya). These women are in different postures and moods, holding different objects:

- Dancing
- Making music with flutes and drums
- Clinging to the branch of a tree
- Carrying water or a basket of food
- Adorning the body

- Being lazy, stretching
- Being angry
- Making garlands
- Holding a mirror
- Shooing away lovers
- Undressing for a lover
- Hunting animals
- Doing martial arts
- Enjoying their body
- Playing with balls
- Playing with birds
- Meditating
- Comforting a baby

Somewhere in between the Buddhist stupa and the Hindu temple, around the tenth century, 1000 years ago, we find a circle of inward-facing women in the Tantrik Age. This was when we started hearing of a superman, who never got exhausted by women, but who exhausted them instead. This was the limitless divine, embodied in Shiva and Vishnu. This was the Tantrik super being, always male, the Siddha.

This was when many circular temples came up in central India, in Madhya Pradesh (Jabalpur, Morena, Khajuraho) and Odisha (Hirapur, Ranipur) and parts of Uttar Pradesh. Many did not survive. Here sixty-four to eighty-four women/goddesses were found. These circles had no roofs. The yogini, we are told, did not like being trapped and was free to fly away when she wished. They were in different forms, different moods, some divine, some demonic, some serene, some maternal, some playful, some domestic, some wild, some violent, some erotic. Some were warriors, some dancers, some musicians. Some were fierce, some gentle, some demure. Some had animal heads, some rode animals, some battled buffalos, lions and elephants. Some had two arms, some multiple arms. Some were terrifying, some were alluring.

These women surrounded Bhairava, a rather fierce form of Shiva, covered with ash and bedecked with skulls, his hair matted. The mood in the yogini circle was eerie and mystical. There was the howling of dogs and wolves, and the cackling of ghosts. No one dared come near this space at night, except those who wished to be part of this occult world. The yogini fed on male virility. She had the power to drive men mad, strip them of all energy. But the man prevailed.

Bhairava satisfied and exhausted the yoginis but remained unexhausted. He was the primal Siddha, who could not be enchanted by anyone. He was a yogi, with control over his mind and senses, not a bhogi, who consumed mental and sensory stimuli.

Unlike earlier tapasvis who could be overpowered by apsaras, the Siddha–Bhairava could overpower the yogini, with full mastery over his sexual fluids. Similar stories are found in Tantrik Buddhist lore, though here Bhairava is replaced by Heruka, a fierce form of the Buddha. Nath Yogi lore also speaks of similar situations, only instead of a circle of women, they speak of a forest of women.

Ancient Indian folklore speaks of an enchanted forest of women where even men turned into women. Such a forest was first mentioned in the Mahabharata, where Prince Sudyumna became a woman called Ila when he entered the forest where Goddess Shakti was enjoying the company of Shiva.

> Hanuman and Matsyendranath were able to enter the enchanted forest of women, without becoming women. The women begged them to stay and give them children. Hanuman refused, as he had chosen the path of restraint and celibacy. Matsyendranath agreed and got trapped in the forest, in the householder's life. His student, Gorakhnath, entered this forest, disguised as a woman, and convinced his teacher to leave the forest. He mocked his guru's entrapment in the household of women. Using his Siddha powers, Gorakhnath killed and revived the guru's son, Minanath, several times. Thus he demonstrated the power of those

who withhold their semen and shun the trap of women. They have no need for the mundane world of household: women, family and children. Gorakhnath finally convinced Matsyendranath to leave his wife and return to the monastic world. Even Minanath followed his father. The women are thus abandoned to live in the world of sensual pleasure and mortality.

This is a Tantrik version of the old Buddhist and Jain tale of a monk who left his family and material world behind. Here sex was explicit. A distinction was made between erotic pleasure and reproductive function. The men satisfied the women but did not shed semen. The unshed semen gave them superhuman power, especially when they used their virility to satisfy fierce women and domesticate them as they once seduced hermits of yore. Here, the male sexual fluid was not split; the man absorbed the sexual fluid of women, reversing the pattern. This was the power of Bhairava and Heruka. And later, the power of the eighty-four Buddhist Maha-siddha, venerated in the Himalayan region, in Vajrayana Buddhist texts. These Siddhas lacked the serenity of monks. They were fierce, engaged in sexual and violent activity, associated with magic and lived in polluted spaces, full of corpses, like battlefields, and burial and cremation grounds.

The strident art involving circles of women waned with the arrival of Islam in India. From around this time, we stopped seeing inscriptions of offerings made to Buddhist, Jain and Hindu establishments by rich independent women. Images of naked bold women, at ease with themselves, were replaced by images of saintly women longing for gods who were almost always embodied in male form, either as Shiva or Vishnu, Rama or Krishna. The Goddess was allowed to appear only as a mother. In many householder traditions, only Bhairava's head was worshipped, not the body. The yogi head was valued over the bhogi body. In these traditions, the female was visualized as a prepubescent child, stripped of sexual and violent energy of the wild yogini.

Radha and her milkmaids appeared in the intersection between the Tantrik and the Bhakti Ages. Like the Tantrik yoginis, the milkmaids faced inwards, towards Krishna. They did not see themselves as temptations, who needed to turn away. They did not see themselves as ravenous consumers of male energy. Nor do they seek exhaustion from the inexhaustible yogis. They simply wanted to enjoy and be enjoyed. This love is not a combat or conquest; it is play.

The circle of milkmaids dancing around Krishna is structurally very similar to the circle of nakshatras around Chandra, the circle of pleasure women around the Buddha and the circle of yoginis dancing around Bhairava and Heruka. But the mood is different. It is full of joy and delight. Women leave the safety of the village of their own free will and risk everything to be in the wilderness, at night, for their own pleasure. Krishna makes all of them happy. Krishna disappears when the women become possessive. When they let go of attachment, he multiplies himself and satisfies all, completely. Having learnt this, they express through the body of Radha the idea that they belong to another (*parakiya*).

In folk songs, which are far more explicit than refined Sanskrit works, Radha is older than Krishna, married to another, her mother's brother, say some songs. Their public union is never possible. It is always a secret, invisible, in the dark, at night, away from social gaze. So Radha is not possessive. She is very unlike Lakshmi, Vishnu's consort, who got angry when Jagannath left the temple without her, who damaged Jagannath's chariot and demanded she return home.

In temples, Lakshmi is always smaller than Vishnu in form. But Radha is always Krishna's equal. In the first third of the Gita Govinda, he is the dominant one. In the second third of the Gita Govinda, they quarrel, separate from and pine for each other. In the final third of the Gita Govinda, when they unite, she is the dominant one, seated atop him. It is the only position that demonstrates female volition in art.

In the gently sloped *chala* temples of Bengal, built around the seventeenth and eighteenth centuries, a special room (*ratna mahal*) was made atop the main room (*garbha griha*) of the deity. Here the mobile images of Radha and Krishna would be taken on special days and placed on a swing. Devotees would sing verses of the Gita Govinda in the courtyard around the temple. In the lower hall, the images on the walls would depict Radha and Krishna separately, their heads and limbs tilting towards each other but never touching each other. In the upper hall, the images would depict Radha and Krishna intertwined to form a single body.

The circle of women draw attention to the feminine world of sensuality and mortality that as per Indian lore the man seeks to escape. We can argue the women here are not women, but metaphors for material reality.

The spirit, or man, yearns for freedom. In the monastic world of Buddhism and Jainism he renounces family, relationships, all pleasure, even food and clothing. In the occult world of Tantra, he becomes the Siddha, who, along with control over his body fluids, gains control over space and time, and has the power to reshape reality as per his whim.

- In the monastic world, women's bodies are seen as gateways to the world of misery and death.

- In the Tantric world, women's bodies are seen as instruments to harness magical powers.

Only in the story of Radha and Krishna we find power being replaced by love. There was a collaborative, friendly and loving relationship between the circle of milkmaids and Krishna. While the yoginis wanted to control Bhairava and Bhairava wanted to escape the yoginis, in the story of the milkmaids and Krishna, we find they gave power to each other. Krishna wanted to make the women happy. The women wanted Krishna to be happy.

Before images of the rasa-mandala or circle of women around Krishna became famous in the sixteenth century, most temples showed images of another episode of Krishna's life. When he stole their clothes when they were bathing in the Yamuna or when he stopped them from selling milk in markets, or when he stole their butter, or trapped them on a boat midstream. These were tales of flirtation, where we are told the women participated as much as Krishna. Flirtation is a game of lovers where each one pretends there are boundaries and hierarchies. The point of the game is not to take power, but to give power.

Yet in the twenty-first century, people argue that such flirtation is actually oppression, abuse disguised as teasing. In effect, the *vastra-haran* (stealing of clothes) of Radha by Krishna enabled the vastra-haran of Draupadi by the Kauravas. Such arguments strip women of power and agency. It assumes power is a limited resource cornered by man. That women do not enjoy the pleasure of flirtation. That romance and flirtation are predatory. Such arguments come from a world where women are Eve and Pandora, not from the world of *Radha Tantra*, composed about 400 years ago, probably in Bengal.

Vishnu came to Shiva to seek a sacred formula or mantra for power. He chanted it in Kashi, but it did not work. So he returned to Mount Kailasa.

This time, the Goddess appeared in front of him, for Shiva was absent. She appeared as Tripura Sundari or Mahamaya, a combination of Lakshmi, Saraswati and Durga, the Goddesses of wealth, knowledge and power. She told Vishnu that using the formula was not enough as it only worked on the mind. He needed to complement the formula by using his body too. For that he needed the help of a willing partner. She thus introduced him to Tantra. She gave Vishnu a beautiful lotus garland. On his way to Vaikuntha, the garland fell on earth, at Vrindavan, in the fragrant tulsi forest on the banks of the dark Yamuna River, and transformed into Radha. Vrindavan was the place where Sati's hair had fallen, when Shiva had carried her corpse in his grief. Vrindavan was where the lotus garland fell and Radha was born. She then awaited the arrival of Vishnu in his mortal form, Krishna. Krishna arrived here and encountered the older, wiser Radha and fell in love. There was playful banter between them, which led to her becoming his guru in the Tantric rites.

Eventually, Radha told Krishna it was time for him to leave Vrindavan, it was time for him to leave Madhuban to go on his adventures. He was meant for other things beyond the village. Krishna therefore left Madhuban for Mathura. He then went to Dwarka and then to Kurukshetra, into the world of men and kings, where he composed the Bhagavad Gita. But he always remembered Radha, the woman who gave him freedom. She told him he was like a butterfly that moved from flower to flower, and she was like the flower that was stuck to the branch of a tree. She would receive the love of Krishna, transform into a fruit and within the fruit would be the seed that would bear another tree. On that tree would be more flowers that would give joy to more butterflies and more birds like Krishna. She would give and he would receive. They would exchange energies with each other and would not try to control each other. Krishna would not seek to control her and she would not seek to control him. This is the world of freedom that we find in Radha's tale.

With the arrival of Radha, the concept of love took centre stage. This was missing in earlier traditions, which focused on power and control. They even focused on knowledge, but they did not focus on the intimacy that came with love. Radha introduces intimacy and love into the narrative. The circle of women is about love, about desire, without seeking control. That is why during the Ratha Yatra festival, we hear how Krishna is returning to Vrindavan.

As per the Bhagavata Purana, when Radha let Krishna go, Krishna left for Mathura on a chariot. All the gopikas wept, but they did not stop him. Krishna promised to return but could not return. Life's journey took him to different places, and he could never come back to Madhuban. That is why, every year, during the Rath Yatra, Jagannath makes it a point to sit on his chariot and return to Vrindavan, for a few nights. On these nights, there is no Lakshmi by his side. The devadasis apply sandal paste on his body, cooling the heat of his passion. During the final three days, after promising Lakshmi that he will return to his temple, he dances with Radha to his heart's content, before resuming his journey south, back to Mathura, to Dwarka, to Kurukshetra.

It was in Madhuban that Krishna discovered love and realized that it was about giving power to people. It was not about controlling them. It was not about holding them. It was not about binding them as daughters, wives, mothers, sisters, but about liberating them as people. The circle of ganikas, of nakshatras, of yoginis, and finally of gopikas, remind us of the wheel of repetitive patterns that delude us, of the inward spiral of entrapment and misery, and the outward spiral of freedom and delight.

All temples in India have the image of a circle of women. But only in Radha's circle Krishna transformed into Purushottama, the perfect man. Krishna, the Purushottama, wore women's clothes and a nose ring. He applied *alta* on his hands, braided his hair in a plait and had no problems wearing women's garments. He knew the complete man was someone who embraced his masculine and feminine sides, stepping in and out with the ease of wearing and discarding clothes. The point is to indulge the other and teach them to indulge you. He thus became the hallmark of feminism.

Devdutt Pattanaik

Source Materials

*Image of the Mother-Goddess created by placing a
metal head, or coconut, on top of a painted pot, or basket,
filled with grain and gold.*

Appleton, Naomi. *Narrating Karma and Rebirth: Buddhist and Jain Multi-Life Stories*. USA: Cambridge University Press, 2014.

Appleton, Naomi. *Shared Characters in Jain, Buddhist and Hindu Narrative: Gods, Kings and Other Heroes (Dialogues in South Asian Traditions: Religion, Philosophy, Literature and History)*. London: Routledge, 2017.

Bolon, Carol Radcliffe. *Forms of the Goddess Lajja Gauri in Indian Art*. Motilal Banarsidass Publishing House, 1996.

Bulcke, C.; Prasāda, D. *Rāmakathā and Other Essays*. Delhi: Vani Prakashan, 2010.

Cabezón, José Ignacio. *Sexuality in Classical South Asian Buddhism (Studies in Indian and Tibetan Buddhism Book 20)*. Wisdom Publications, 2017.

Kinsley, David R. *Hindu Goddesses*. Motilal Banarsidass, 1986.

De, Sushil Kumar. *Ancient Indian Erotics and Erotic Literature*. Kolkata: Firma K.L. Mukhopadhayay, 1969.

Bryant, Edwin Francis. *Krishna: A Sourcebook*. Suny Press, 2007.

Ganguli, Kisari Mohan (trans.). *The Mahabharata of Krishna: Kisari Mohan Ganguli's Translation of the Epic Indian Saga* (ten volumes). New Delhi: Prabhat Prakashan, 2017.

Gokhale, Namita; Lal, Malasri (ed.). *In Search of Sita: Revisiting Mythology*. India: Penguin Books Limited, 2009.

Beck, Guy. *Alternative Krishnas: Regional and Vernacular Variations on a Hindu Deity*. SUNY Press, 2005.

Haksar, Aditya Narayan Dhairyasheel. *Shuka Saptati: Seventy Tales of the Parrot*. India: HarperCollins India, 2000.

Hawley, John Stratton; Wulff, Donna Marie, eds. *The Divine Consort: Rādhā and the Goddesses of India*. Berkeley Religious Studies Series, 3. Berkeley, Ca: Graduate Theological Union, 1982.

Hayes, Glen Alexander. 'Contemporary Metaphor Theory and Alternative Views of Krishna and Rādhā in Vaishnava Sahajiyā'. In

Guy L. Beck (ed.). *Alternative Krishnas: Regional and Vernacular Variations on a Hindu Deity. Albany*, NY: SUNY Press, 2005.

Hiltebeitel, Alf. *Cult of Draupadi, Mythologies from Gingee to Kuruksetra.* USA: University of Chicago Press, 1998.

Hiltebeitel, Alf. *Rethinking India's Oral and Classical Epics: Draupadi among Rajputs, Muslims, and Dalits.* University of Chicago Press, 1999. Reprinted Delhi: Oxford, 2001.

Jain, Meenakshi (ed.). *Sati: Evangelicals, Baptist Missionaries, and the Changing Colonial Discourse.* New Delhi: Aryan Books International, 2016.

Kocchar, Rajesh. *The Vedic People: Their History and Geography.* New Delhi: Orient Blackswan, 2001.

Kramrisch, S. *The Presence of Siva.* USA: The Princeton/Bollingen Series in World, 1981.

Mani, Vettam. *Puranic Encyclopedia: A Comprehensive Work with Special Reference to the Epic and Puranic Literature.* New Delhi: Motilal Banarsidass, 2015.

McDaniel, June. 'The Tantric Rādhā'. *Journal of Vaishnava Studies*, 2000.

Menzies, Jackie. *Goddess: Divine Energy.* Art Gallery of New South Wales, 2006.

Meyer, Johann Jakob. *Sexual Life In Ancient India: A Study in the Comparative History of Indian Culture.* New Delhi: Motilal Banarsidass Publishing House, 1971

Miller, Barbara S. 'Rādhā: Consort of Kṛṣṇa's Vernal Passion'. *Journal of the American Oriental Society*, 1975.

Mohan, Peggy. *Wanderers, Kings, Merchants: The Story of India through Its Languages.* New Delhi: Penguin Random House India, 2021.

Mulchandani, Sandhya. *Erotic Literature Of Ancient India: 'Kama Sutra', 'Koka Shastra', 'Gita Govindam', 'Ananga Ranga'.* India: Roli, 2007.

Olivelle, Patrick. *A Dharma Reader: Classical Indian Law (Historical Sourcebooks in Classical Indian Thought)*. USA: Columbia University Press, 2017.

Olivelle, Patrick. *Grhastha: The Householder in Ancient Indian Religious Culture*. London: Oxford University Press, 2019.

Burchett, Patton E. *A Genealogy of Devotion: Bhakti, Tantra, Yoga, and Sufism in North India*. New York: Columbia University Press, 2019.

Possehl, Gregory L. *The Indus Civilization: A Contemporary Perspective*. AltaMira Press, 2002.

Powers, John. *A Bull of a Man: Images of Masculinity, Sex, and the Body in Indian Buddhism*. Cambridge, Mass.: Harvard University Press, 2009.

Richman, Paula (ed.). *Many Ramayanas: The Diversity of a Narrative Tradition in South Asia*. United Kingdom: University of California Press, 1991.

Richman, Paula (ed.). *Questioning Ramayanas: A South Asian Tradition*. United Kingdom: University of California Press, 2001.

Sethi, Manisha. *Escaping the World: Women Renouncers among Jains (South Asian History and Culture)*. New Delhi: Taylor and Francis, 2012.

Soneji, Davesh. *Unfinished Gestures: Devadasis, Memory, and Modernity in South India*. London: University of Chicago Press, 2012.

Srivastava, A.L. *Uma-Mahesvara (An Iconographic Study of the Divine Couple)*. India: Sukarkshetra Shodh Sansthan, 2004.

Thapar, Romila. *Sakuntala: Texts, Readings, Histories*. New York: Columbia University Press, 2011.

White, Charles S.J. *The Caurāsī Pad of Śrī Hit Harivaṃś: Introduction, Translation, Notes, and Edited Braj Bhaṣa*. Asian Studies at Hawaii, 16. Honolulu: University Press of Hawaii, 1977.

Whitehead, Henry. *The Village Gods of South India*. London: Associated Press, 1921.

Young, Serinity. *Courtesans and Tantric Consorts: Sexualities in Buddhist Narrative, Iconograhy, and Ritual.* New York and London: Routledge, 2004.

Scan QR code to access the
Penguin Random House India website